STOCKPORT
BY GASLIGHT

STOCKPORT
BY GASLIGHT

Harry Littlewood

Edited by Joss Carpreau

from the posts on Stockport Memories and Memories of Stockport

Facebook pages

Elephant Memoirs

Edited and designed by Elephant Memoirs
www.elephant-memoirs.co.uk
Printed by Book Printing UK

British Library CIP data: a catalogue record for this book is available
from the British Library.

ISBN   978-1-8383332-0-1

Picture Credits
Cover photo (Bridgefield Street) Stockport Local Heritage Library
Map copyright of Ordnance Survey and www.old-maps.co.uk
Page 3 Hilary M Battersby
Page 5 Christine Emmons
Page 63 Unknown author cc by-sa
Page 69 Unknown author cc by-sa
Page 121 Niall Dorsett cc by-sa
Page 125 Michael Danyliw
Page 131 Unknown author cc by-sa
Back cover (Harry Littlewood) Christine Emmons

All other images used by permission of Stockport Local Heritage
Library

Contents

THE BRIDGEFIELD AREA OF STOCKPORT IN THE 1950s.

PREFACE

Harry Littlewood was in his sixties when he started writing about his younger years growing up in the slums of Stockport. His posts for Stockport Memories and Memories of Stockport on Facebook had hundreds of followers. Between 2014 and 2019 he wrote nearly fifty accounts of growing up in Stockport in the 1950s. He did so with such passion and remembrance that many a loyal reader encouraged him to write this book.

The inspiration for Harry's writing was the area of Stockport that used to be called Bridgefield. Hardly anyone knows where that is anymore because starting in 1959 the entire area was demolished. Stockport Council's slum clearance scheme knocked down all the streets between the existing Prince's Street and the red rocks lining the M60 motorway. An entire community was wiped out over the course of about a year.

At first, the Council built the Great Egerton Street car parks over the Bridgefield neighbourhood. In 2015, however, these were dug up and the Red Rock leisure complex was built. The site of the courtyard where Harry lived now lies under the cinema.

Sadly, Harry Littlewood died in November 2019, and never got to see this book before it was completed. It has been incredibly important to his youngest daughter to see that it is finished. His memories have been collated and edited into separate chapters, each with a different subject.
Joss Carpreau, Elephant Memoirs

FOREWORD

The redevelopment site underneath the Bridgefield Street carparks.
The Red Rock leisure complex was built over the top in 2016.

I f you remember, earlier this year I collected the old toilet that was found in one of the courtyards that had been excavated on the Bridgefield estate. This land was about to be built over, with the Red Rock development. Although this loo was not in our courtyard, it was in a courtyard I had been in many times. I used this loo on many occasions as a kid. I worked in the shop on the corner of Woodman Street and Great Egerton Street, cleaning and stacking shelves for Mrs Cook. The toilet was at the back of the shop in the courtyard. It was the first one on the row, but most toilets were shared then.

Strange after all those years how it came to the surface. And I spotted it. This loo must be about a hundred and fifty years old, as the houses were built around 1820 to 1840. It had lain under the tarmac of the car parks for sixty-odd years, and that's when I last used it as a nipper. There was not a great deal of damage to it, considering how old it was, and it even had half the wooden seat still left on it.

I used to stone this toilet cubicle every week for Mrs Cook. I can see myself on my hands and knees with a bucket of water, a couple of donkey stones and a floor cloth. You could get the stones off the rag-bone man, but Mrs Cook also sold them, in about three to four different colours. My mother taught me how to stone steps when I was about six years old. I used to love doing our toilet and the front doorstep and a few flags under the window in Robin Court, making pretty patterns with them. I wonder how many donkey stones there are left today, and who even knows how to do it anymore?

The old, cobbled courtyard at the back of the shop is where the toilet I used many times stood. One of my Saturday jobs was to clean the toilet, so it should have still recognised me last week, as I had once looked after it. I even used to cream-stone a fancy border on the floor inside the cellar.

The toilet looks well in my garden now and is a constant reminder of the days I spent in the slums of Old Stockport Town.

Harry Littlewood, 2016

Harry Littlewood collecting the old toilet from the Great Egerton Street car park development. February 2016.

INTRODUCTION

Bridgefield and Stockport from Lancashire Hill.

Stockport town centre is now predominantly a shopping area, with little residential accommodation in comparison to how it was before 1960. Very few people live in the Bridgefield area or even know where it is any more. Whereas Merseyway precinct is now the main shopping area, when I was growing up it was Prince's Street shared with Portwood and the Underbanks. Either side of Prince's Street and surrounding areas consisted of row upon row of brick-built terraced houses. I spent the first ten years of my life on the Bridgefield estate, in a little courtyard called Robin Court, just off Brown Street. Brown Street is still there but after the slum clearance of the early sixties, the entire Bridgefield estate was earmarked for re-development. Where my house used to stand, they built car parks for the Merseyway shopping precinct. The other side of Great Egerton Street, they built the M60 motorway. Where the Red Rock cinema, restaurants and gym now stand was just a small part of the slums of Old Stockport Town, and is where I started my life in the 1940s.

Stockport was in full swing in its heyday. The factories and cotton mills were working flat out, and no one was ever out of work as the mills steamed ahead, producing millions of yards of cotton, for home and export. Stockport was also never a single industry town. Hatting was also one of Stockport's exports, and over six million hats a year were manufactured here.

It may seem hard to believe that on these roads around Brinksway, Hillgate, Great Egerton Street and Bridgefield stood several hundred dilapidated terraced houses that were occupied by the workforce that kept the wheels of the cotton industry of Stockport turning. Up to the 1960s, the centre of Stockport from Hillgate to Heaton Norris, and Brinksway to Portwood, was very densely populated, and hordes of mill workers and their families lived and worked there, including mine. Families were crowded together in narrow cobbled streets in brick houses, blackened with decades of grime, soot and smoke that belched daily from the local factory chimneys. I can clearly remember the mill workers, young and old alike, in their turbans, curlers and clogged feet. I can still hear their clogs clattering on the pavement and cobbles as they made their way to the gloomy, hot, noisy mills of Stockport. They toiled away the long hours of the day for a pittance of pay.

I remember the houses where my playmates lived, and the little corner shops where I spent my pennies, I remember them all so well. The shopping streets were full of life, the market was always bursting at the seams, and sometimes the pace would be down to a shuffle as you made your way through the crowds. Those communities were the lifeblood of Stockport and kept its heart beating until the slum clearance of the 1960s. Stockport had its fair share of old, run down, and overcrowded dwellings in the 1950s, just as most towns did. The houses were predominantly populated by the more unfortunate and underprivileged members of society.

I was born in 1948 on a very cold January night, so I was told. I slowly became aware of my surroundings as a child, and I remember the little one-up one-down house where I was to spend the next ten years of my childhood. That childhood left many deep-rooted memories that were made over seven decades ago. It never occurred to me that I lived in a slum area, because everywhere I looked appeared to be the same. Row upon row of old terraced houses adorned the quaint cobbled streets of my home town. I remember the litter-free streets, the doorsteps cleaned and donkey-stoned weekly, and the white net curtains draped inside the sparkling clean windows of the homes. They were houseproud residents who lived on the Bridgefield estate.

Not many 'well off' people lived on the estate and anyone who had a few bob did not live in Bridgefield. The people here didn't have much, and lacked many of the material possessions of life, but pride and self-respect more than filled that void.

Never once, at any stage in my young life, did I ever feel as though I needed or wanted for anything, or was in any way put at a disadvantage by my upbringing in the slums of Old Stockport Town. It wasn't until years later I realised I was one of the many kids of that era who'd been brought up in poverty. I also realised, however, that I was privileged to have been raised by such warm-hearted people. Tremendous love and affection existed in those close-knit communities and in the face of harsh and adverse living conditions and the poverty we endured, there was awe-inspiring friendliness and a tremendous sense of pride and self-respect amongst the residents. I have always felt proud to have been a part of that community.

I remember the good community spirit where everyone was always cheerful in spite of the grim future we all faced. It was only sheer determination and hard work that helped many of us poorer families to survive the hardships we all endured. Such was this close-knit community of caring warm-hearted people, who always helped, respected and trusted one another. No one was ever left alone in time of need, and believe me, that was more often than not.

When I look back at my childhood days, by and large I see them as the happiest days of my life. But of course, then we had no cares or worries, as our parents did all the worrying for us. Our only concern was getting out to play with our playmates. I remember Stockport how it used to be in the fifties, and I loved every minute of it as a kid. Seen through the eyes of a child it was just a big adventure playground, a world away from how our parents saw it.

The word 'nostalgia' describes a longing for the past or a longing for home or familiar surroundings. Someone once said,

'Nostalgia is wishful thinking in reverse, a recollection of distant memories that causes everything in the past to seem better than it actually was.' Everyone has memories of their days gone by, particularly their childhood, and those are the memories we treasure throughout our lives. What we remember from our childhood we remember forever. And the good times leave the greatest impression on us. We tend to forget the rest.

However, if you talk to the older generation today, they rarely convey a true impression of life in the fifties. Most say life was better then: life had a slower pace than today, people had time for each other and were more neighbourly, there was less crime, drunkenness, violence, selfishness and greed, and everything about modern-day life is so stressful now. I agree with most of this, but people seem to forget how difficult life was for so many of the larger families that lived hand-to-mouth from one payday to the next.

The world's changed a lot since the fifties: some say for the better, some say for the worse, but whichever way, we can't turn the clock back. My life spent in Old Stockport Town holds some very fond memories for me and I often take walks down 'memory lane', remembering the times when my family were still together. But I have no wish to return to the dark days and the terrible conditions of the 1950 that I spent my childhood in.

Having been earmarked for re-development, the slum clearance campaign of the Bridgefield estate began in 1957. The oldest and most run-down houses began to disappear under Stockport Borough's slum clearance program. Whole swathes of these terraced houses were demolished and many of the residents were put into high-rise flats. However, those flats eventually proved to be very unpopular with many people, particularly the older generation of the time. The old, terraced houses may have been grim but at least they had a strong sense of community.

For the last sixty years, the land between Great Egerton Street and Bridgefield Street, the streets I roamed during my childhood, was used as car parks. The houses were swept away long ago, the residents gone and forgotten. The homes that stood on those streets were reduced to brick and dust sixty years ago, and that included the one I lived in. It was a sad day when those houses came down, as a big part of my life went with them. As I stood and watched them fall, tears came to my eyes. They were slums, but I didn't know that then. All I knew then was that they were my home, my town. It wasn't a sight for the faint-hearted as my hometown was bulldozed into something that resembled a war zone. All my friends and neighbours were dispersed far afield across Stockport. We had lived our lives together, played together, worked together. And now they were gone.

Sadly, as the years rolled by to the present day, I watched the face of Stockport change beyond all recognition. In 2018 the car parks were replaced by the cinemas and restaurants of the Red Rock complex. Sometimes though, as I walk the same paths where I spent my childhood and retrace the footsteps I made more than half a century ago, I am oblivious to the changes that have taken place around me. I see only the shadows of my childhood past. I hear the laughter once again resonating around the spaces where those houses once stood. I hear my name being called to play once again, echoing in the distance. I hear the voices of those that I have loved and lost. And as the tears well up in my eyes, I pause for a moment to think of all those whom I shared my childhood with, and all those who have gone before me. The wonderful times and the lasting memories of childhood, I still cherish today. And shall forever.

I look back, not with a nostalgic sense of the good old days, as that they certainly weren't, but for me, my parents and the other residents that lived in this part of Stockport between the fifties and the slum clearance of the sixties, this book shows an insight into what life was really like.

A WALK AROUND BRIDGEFIELD

Bridgefield Street looking from the A6 end.

All those years ago, I never thought I would see anything built on the grounds where I used to live. Back then it was just rows and rows of old terraced houses that lined the cobbled streets of this grimy cotton mill town. How times change, and how time flies. It doesn't seem all that long ago that I lived only a few yards from the new Red Rock complex.

Red Rock is now open, but what was there before? Where Red Rock stands now was just a small part of the slums of Old Stockport Town, and is where I started my life in 1948. I was brought up in these back-street slums in a little cobbled courtyard directly in front of where Red Rock leisure complex is today. Bridgefield Street stands on one side of the complex and Great Egerton Street stands on the other, and Brown Street and Woodman Street still link the two. I remember only too well how our life was spent on that estate, and six of us lived in cramped conditions in a one-up and one-down back-to-back house.

I went into Stockport a while back but as I had a bit of a wait, I got a Cornish pasty and went back to the car on the Great Egerton Street car park for a snack. I had a good view from where I was sitting and looking up and down this street, where I once played as a kid, my mind's eye started putting the houses back where they had once stood sixty-odd years ago. I knew those streets like the back of my hand, and almost everyone that lived in them in the 1950s.

I was watching people walking back and to, going about their business, and thinking to myself, 'I'm sure you didn't realise that was Mrs Randal's living room you've just walked through.' Mrs Randal was an old dear who lived on Great Egerton Street and once pawned a 'tater pie at Corbishley's pawn shop on Egerton Street. It then dawned on me that I had parked in the corner shop on Woodman Street, the shop that I'd spent so much time in as a kid with the wonderful Mrs Cook. This kind lady shopkeeper had taken an under-privileged kid on a day's outing to Blackpool to see the Illuminations. I'd never seen the sea or been on a 'charabanc' before. These were long open-topped single-decker buses, with canvas hoods for if it rained, which it often did in Blackpool. We had fish and chips sitting on a bench on the seafront. What a memorable day that was. A day never to be forgotten.

So I sat in the car for the next hour, 'walking' down memory lane, remembering all the houses that had once stood in this part of Old Stockport Town, and the people who had lived in them. I could feel those streets once again beneath my feet, the very same streets I had once played on. I remembered those hot summer days we spent sat on the kerb popping the tar bubbles that used to appear, and picking the 'gas tar' from between the cobbles to make little balls with. When you look down some of those streets on the old photos, the absence of litter is testament to the fact that the residents kept it clean and clear of rubbish.

I stopped periodically to gaze over the landscape now before me. All I saw were cars parked on the grounds where those terraced houses were many years ago. I remembered the names of some of the residents that had lived there (the Durrs, Carters, Boswells, Dooleys, the Barratts, Ogdens, Harrisons, Dyers and many more) and put them all back in their respective homes.

I could pinpoint the exact spot on Brown Street where our house had once stood over half a century ago. Here the family would sit by gaslight at night to eat and we kids would try to read our comics in the poor light that the gas gave off. It seems such a long time ago, but I grew up in an era where gas lamps still lit the paths we walked in the centre of town. I remember walking the gas-lit streets at night, into the blackness before me, the dim glow of each gaslight an eerie sight peering out from the mist or drizzle. As I approached the light, I could hear the hissing of the burning gas, and see my shadow cast on the pavement.

Stockport had many a dull day from the pollution we produced by our coal-fired homes and factories. On winter days, a dark cloud would hang above Stockport. Walking around the streets, I'd see the cobbles twinkling like little diamonds in the rain, the wet slate rooves reflecting the light back up under the grey skies. Each and every house had a chimney with a column of smoke rising through the drizzling rain into the air, adding more obnoxious fumes to the already polluted atmosphere.

Now as I walked past Brown Street, where I had once lived, I looked towards where our house once stood. I remembered my father and mother, and how they struggled to make a living, and thought of my three siblings, of whom only one is now left. My eyes filled up, and a tear trickled down my face. So many memories to contend with. Now, the street was virtually empty and there was hardly anyone around. It was just so sad to see it lifeless and soulless like that. I left thinking I'd seen enough and I really didn't want to be there anymore. I said a silent hello and thank you to all those who had lived there and made my life such a joy in the slums of Old Stockport Town.

As I took this walk, I become ever more nostalgic and tainted with sadness. As the shadows of my past appeared before me, I remembered the strong, loving communities that I was brought up in all those years ago. The streets as I remember them are still there, but the houses that stood on them and the people I knew that lived in them are long gone. How I would love to go back. Just for a day.

WE SHOPPED ON A DAILY BASIS

Ellis Sykes on Prince's Street.

Stockport will always be a place I remember with great fondness and affection. I spent the first ten years of my life in the back-street slums of this smoky old town. It was a childhood that left many deep-rooted memories: memories formed more than six decades ago that are still as clear today as they were then.

Another time when I went to Stockport a while back, I sat outside a café and remembered the trams trundling up Prince's Street to Mersey Square. I had come in the car and parked directly outside where the Prince's Picture House on Prince's Street once was, just like I could have done almost seventy years ago. It never occurred to me then as a kid, that almost seven decades later I would be parking my own car right behind myself on that very same street. I remembered the Prince's cinema well, only Poundland stands in its place now. I remembered standing in the doorway of this once proud picture house in 1952. It was very eerie. I recalled the foyer full of dust and paper that had blown in from the street. And that unique smell of popcorn that we got with the cinemas was oozing from inside. The closed and disused cinema now stood empty and deserted. The last film to be shown was pasted on the boards inside, but never again were those seats to fill another house. Time and technology had finally caught up with it, just as they had with the Palladium further down Prince's Street.

What a strange feeling it was. I was overcome by a great wave of nostalgic emotion. I then walked along Prince's Street. I was dismayed, to say the least, at how Prince's Street has changed so much from how I remember it as a nipper. This used to be the main shopping area back then, along with the Underbanks, and the market that was on two days a week.

I remember Price's bakery, which was originally Rudd's. They had their bakery on Woodman Street just over the road. One thing we found out as kids, to our delight, was that Rudd's never locked the back door of the bakery at night, for some strange reason. One or two of the more adventurous kids used to squeeze under the gate of the garage where the bakery parked their van, and go through the bakehouse door at night. They'd come out with a box of half a dozen cakes and maybe a couple of chocolate dolls. Needless to say, I always helped them to demolish their ill-gotten gains, sat on the steps on Brown Street that led up to Stewart Street.

I now walked past the UCP over the road and really thought I could still smell those wonderful fish 'n' chips wafting along Prince's Street. I remember the UCP on Prince's Street with great fondness as I used to buy some of their wonderful chips to eat as I walked along, if I had a few pennies to spare for a portion. They were never wrapped in newspaper like the chippies did, but were put into a greaseproof bag. On a Friday night, Mum used to send me to the back door of the UCP on Bridgefield Street for a bob's worth of chips for our teas. We got a lot then for a bob because although chips were thre'pence a portion at the chippies, we got a better deal at the UCP. But by the time I got home there were never quite as many as there should have been, and I had grease all round my face.

Walking down the ginnel between the UCP and the Swan With Two Necks, as I did many times in the fifties, the stench of people blatantly and obviously using it as a toilet was gross. I remembered the Palladium picture house on the corner of Hatton Street, with the art deco walls at the side, and I saw it was still there. It had stood empty for a good few years, but later became Henry's Stores and Sunspot Supermarket in the early sixties. At Hollingdrakes (now rebuilt) we kids would go inside at around five o'clock in the evening, and sit on the stairs to watch *Popeye* on the display TV. The staff always let us, and never bothered us until it was over, but then they would move us on.

Lowes, the bakers, was a place where I could guarantee to get a free cake from. I used to go in with tuppence and ask if they had any broken cakes. One woman in there had a heart of gold and must have always felt sorry for me. Mind you, I was only seven at the time. If she didn't have any cakes, she would deliberately break a couple of vanillas or a couple of rock cakes, put them in a bag and say, "Hurry up before the Old Crow comes out." She meant the manageress, and what a mean old crow she was too, but the woman never took my money off me. I could also get a crusty dinner cob for one penny, or three ha'pence if you wanted it buttered, from Robinsons next to Boots Chemist in Mersey Square.

Woolworths, where we used to admire all the toys, with no money in our pockets to buy, was now boarded up. Meesons, the sweet shop where I used to go for my gran's Mint Imperials, was next door to the Prince's cinema, and I always enjoyed a couple of the mints on my way home, walking down Brown Street. If Gran knew the bag was a bit light, she never said anything, bless her.

I looked across the road to where the corner shop used to stand on Great Egerton Street and Woodman Street. The local corner shops were always a hive of activity, with the local women gossiping to find out what was going on in the neighbourhood. I spent loads of time in that shop as a kid, with the wonderful Mrs Cook. It was one of those marvellous, quaint little corner shops that sold everything you needed, from Beechams back and kidney pills and influenza powders, to the assortment of sweets in the penny liquorice tray. There were cakes, sterilized milk bottles in wooden crates, bread, firewood and firelighters, and not forgetting the tins of 'snuff' next to the packets of cigarettes. I always remember old Tommy coming into the shop from the lodging house further down Great Egerton Street. He came in every night on his way home to the lodging house, but the only thing he ever bought was a Cadburys one penny chocolate bar. He always opened it in the shop and crammed the whole thing in his mouth before leaving, putting the empty foil wrapper in his pocket.

I remembered the times I spent helping to stack the shelves in the corner shop and cleaning the rubber mats that lay on the customers' side of the floor. The mats were large and very heavy, but small as I was I'd drag them outside and lay them on the pavement on Woodman Street then scrub them off with a bucket of warm soapy water from the 'scullery', as Mrs Cook called it. I'd dry them off and take them back in, after mopping the shop floor with a bit of San Izal disinfectant in the bucket. I'd also be the one handling the firelighters, so Mrs Cook didn't have to keep going into the scullery to wash her hands.

I have many memories of the steps down to the scullery, and I can still see myself walking up and down them carrying the bacon or cooked meat. There were no fridges then and keeping the cooked meats, bacon and cheese fresh was difficult, particularly in the warmer weather.

At the bottom of the steps there was a space underneath and in there was a marble slab. I remember how cool the cellar used to be. The cellar was exceptionally clean and was whitewashed all over. A door made of fine wire mesh, to keep out any creepies, covered the entrance to under the stairs.

When a customer wanted bacon or a slice or two of ham or maybe corned beef, I'd be the one to go down and get it. I loved going in there, as the coolness, and the smell of the bacon and cooked meats together was gorgeous. I'd wait until Mrs Cook had finished slicing it, then take it back down to lay on the cool marble slab. The cooked meats always had a sheet of greaseproof paper wrapped around them.

The corner shop was where we shopped on a daily basis because we had no fridges, no frozen food or tempting offers like Buy One Get One Free. You paid (most of the time on tick) only for what you wanted and needed, a slice or two of bacon or maybe a couple of slices of boiled ham for Father's wrap-up. Many times, Mother would send me for an egg (yes, just the one) which the shopkeeper placed in a paper bag and I duly put in my pocket. I took care on the way home not to break it otherwise I'd get a clip round the ear and have to go back to for another.

In most shops you could buy five Park Drive or five Woodbine cigarettes. If Mrs Cook didn't have a five-pack, she would split a ten-pack for you, or even sell you two or three cigs if you were short of money. We could get a Park Drive fag for tuppence, from under the counter. Then she'd put the cigs into one of those cone-shaped toffee bags. No age limits then. Three or four of us would go to smoke them on the Hollow on the Red Rec. That was until someone snitched on us, and a teacher came over the top and caught us all. Didn't stop us, we just found somewhere else. Mrs Cook would also sell you a bottle of cough mixture. Mind you, if we had known then not to buy the fags, there would have been no need for the cough mixture.

How I remember and loved the smells in the corner shop, in particular the soap corner where they kept the soap and soap powders and disinfectants. I especially liked the red Lifebuoy washing soap, which we used in our house as kids. It had a lovely strong scented smell. Dad used it for shaving, Mother used it for washing clothes, and we kids used it for washing ourselves with before going to school. I still use it today, if I can get hold of it.

When I worked at the corner shop, I never got paid in cash, just in kindness or with tea and sandwiches. I would sit on a box in the storeroom at the back of the shop eating the corned beef or ham sandwiches that Mrs Cook had made me, and I got a discount on sweets when I was going to school. The little corner shops opened early in the morning to catch the workers going to work, and the kids going to school spending their pennies. And they stayed open till late in the evening. I remember going home in the dark many a time around nine o'clock. What wonderful memories. Mrs Cook would also give me the cakes that were left at the end of the day to take home and share out among my sibs.

The shop used to be owned by an old couple called Mr and Mrs Whatmough. The Whatmoughs had run the shop for many years. It was our local shop and I went there many times, with a note from Mother to pick up one or two things. One particular day in 1953, I went to the shop and it was closed so I returned home empty-handed. Mother, not believing I had actually been there, then went herself. She returned looking a bit ashen faced.

"The shop is closed, and Mr Whatmough is dead," she said to Dad. "I've just seen Mrs Green opposite and she said she'd heard that Mrs Whatmough had pushed the old man down the cellar steps." And so the rumours began, whether that was intentional or not. However, the shop remained closed for several weeks after this, until it opened under a new name.

Constance Burgess and her husband Bernard were the ones that now owned the shop, but her Mother Mrs Cook, who lived on Alpine Road, actually ran it. She was a lovely, kind-hearted lady who had the time of day for anyone.

One day I was in the storeroom working near the cellar door when Jonathan (Constance's boy) went down to fill a coal scuttle. Once he was out of sight, I hid behind the door on the cellar head until I heard him walking back up the steps. I then let out a ghostly cry as my hand reached round the door to grab him. Well, the scream he let out brought Mrs Cook running from the shop immediately, with a good telling off for me.

And then there were those silly Sunday trading laws we had to endure, where you could buy a quarter of corned beef, but not a tin; a bottle of pasteurised milk, but not sterilised; a cake, but not biscuits. If the shopkeeper knew you well enough, she would sell you anything, and tell you to hide it under your coat or put it in your pocket before leaving the shop, otherwise she would be liable to prosecution. What a difference to today's laws.

A lot of the corner shop customers had a tick-book, a little red one, where they'd write down what they had bought, then would hopefully pay at the weekend. Try doing that in a supermarket. They didn't have calculators or tills that totalled up the purchases, they wrote it down on a piece of paper to total it all up after, and many a mistake was made then.

Now, as I walked down Prince's Street, I looked to the left and I imagined I saw Madam Betty's ladies' garments, and next door to her on the corner of Brown Street was Halfords bicycle shop. This was where I got my puncture repair outfits, so Dad could mend my bike when I was a kid. Just over the road from Halfords on Brown Street was Natco Chambers, and the building is still there. It was run by the same chap who had the health food shop on the ground floor.

This was where Mum sent me to pick up the tins of National Dried Milk (baby food). I loved the taste of this stuff as I sneakily dipped my finger into it. She'd also get free bottles of orange juice and cod liver oil with the milk tokens she used to get. Farley's Rusks, I could eat them all day long. We had to go in the health food shop first with the tokens, then he would take you upstairs to collect the order.

I sat now outside Grandad's Chippy drinking my coffee after finishing my dinner of fish 'n' chips. I looked up and down the street at the cheerless depressing shops that I now saw before me: pawn shops, phone shops, betting shops, money lenders, charity shops, game arcades, and many shops boarded up with To Let signs. I particularly noticed a great absence of people, and it was nothing like the hustle and bustle of the 1950s that I remembered. Stockport always used to be so busy and full of life and was always buzzing with shoppers. You would not have been able to sit outside like I did without getting trampled on.

I remembered at the top of Prince's Street was Boots chemists on the corner with Mersey Square. Mum would send me there for Sulio to treat the head lice with. It was a yellow substance and you'd scream blue murder if it got in your eyes. We'd also get camphor blocks to ease our breathing. In winter, she used to hang them round our necks in little cloth bags that she made.

Next door was Watters Westbrook where I went for Dad's baccy, no questions asked then. Downstairs was the barber where you could get your hair cut. We could never afford to have our hair cut there though, and Mum or Dad used to cut ours. Next door was another entrance to Boots. Then there was Easifit shoe shop. I saw my favourite cake shop of the 1950s,

Lowes, now boarded up and to let. I felt so sad as all the memories of that street in the fifties came back. This was the same cake shop where I used to get my free broken cakes from. Bright House used to be Eastman's butchers, a double-fronted shop that was always really busy. Cunningham's opticians, where I got my first pair of glasses in the fifties, is still there and I still use that opticians today. How's that for loyalty? I only had to go to the end of our street back then.

Evans Bros was the butchers opposite Marks and Spencer's. I remember one of the horrors of the 1950s for me was being sent there by my Dad to get a sheep's head. "Ask him to split it," Dad said. I watched in horror as the butcher brought the axe down on this skinless head, white with red veins and blood running from it, with its eyes bulging and the teeth seemingly grinning at him. I ran home with this thing in my hands holding it well abreast till I got home. And then, I kid ye not, Dad placed it on the table, opened the head and scooped out the brains with a spoon. That's a gruesome picture that has stayed with me to this day. He put the brains in a cloth and boiled the head and brains together in the pan. I couldn't go near the thing: seeing that head bobbing up and down in the boiling water made me sick. Then I saw him make a butty with the brains. Later he would pick the meat off the head while listening to his radio, while I would go out or play upstairs. For crying out loud, Dad, what were you trying to do to me? It is a memory so deeply embedded that I have never forgotten it. But still, the wonderful memories of my childhood also linger on today.

I remembered the grocer's shop on Egerton Street well. I lived at the back of it, and many was the time I would run from the courtyard at the back to go to the shop to pick up some items for Mother. It was one of three grocer's shops on Great Egerton Street, and not the most hygienic. I remember it was a very dim dark place and it had a rather unpleasant smell on entering. It was quite a frightening place for a kid to be in, as I could hear the old woman's heavy clogs scraping along the wooden floor as she made her way into the shop. She would pause in the doorway, holding onto the door frame to steady herself. And with a booming voice she would call out, "Now then!" as if to say, 'What do you want?' After serving you, she would slap your change down on the counter with a fair old thud, which made you jump. Mrs Wild never gave it to you in your hand, as most shopkeepers did. I'd pick it up and run out of the shop like a bat out of hell. One single light bulb over the counter lit the entire shop. It stood in a time zone of its own, and it seemed as though it never moved with time from the day it was built.

Mrs Wild's dog, an Alsatian, always sat on the pavement outside her shop. Mrs Wild was there probably, just inside the doorway, as she never left the dog out on its own. Mrs Wild was a grey-haired toothless old dear with a bun in her hair, a heavily wrinkled face and a long black skirt that stopped short above her ankles. You could just see her metal-studded clogs below. And what a racket they made as she walked along the pavement or past our door in the courtyard to go to the loo. A black lace shawl covered her shoulders, and a leather pinafore hung in front of her black skirt. She used to stand on the shop doorstep quite a lot in the warmer weather. Many a time as I passed by, I'd say hello, but all I got back was a deep inaudible grunt.

Mrs Wild was a very old woman and probably incapable of keeping the place clean and up to a reasonable standard. The place was a two-up and two-down and Mrs Wild lived, and slept, downstairs in the back room. I presume she was too old and frail to make it up and down stairs. The back door of the shop was directly opposite our back door in the courtyard. On many occasions, especially on warm days, as I walked past I'd see the old dear sat on the edge of her bed gazing into space in a world of her own. The hearth in front of the large cast-iron grate would be covered in a pile of ash. The back place where she lived left a lot to be desired.

I remember walking past the shop door one day with my playmate Raymond Ogden, who lived a few doors away. As we walked by, Raymond and I were laughing at something, but Mrs Wild took it the wrong way and thought we were laughing at her. She raised the back of her hand as if to clout us one, and said, "You cheeky little buggers, ge'rout of it!"

I remember one day Mother sending me to Wilds for a bottle of milk. But as I ran back across the courtyard and neared our house, I tripped on one of the uneven flags. I had the bottle by the neck in my left hand and as I fell the bottle smashed and a large sliver of glass almost took my thumb off. I lay on the ground face down, looking at this little river of milk running under my head along the pavement. Slowly it turned pink with streaks of red in it. I remember Mrs Harrison next door coming out to see what the commotion was, and the look of horror on her face as she screamed for Mother. After sixty-three years, I still bear that large scar. In fact, every time I see it, it reminds me of the time I ran through the courtyard.

Hardly anyone had a telephone then so Mother wrapped a towel round my hand, and we ran to the fire station in Mersey Square, because they would know more about first aid there than she did. The towel by then was soaked in blood as we arrived. One of the duty firemen took one look at it, wrapped it back up and took me and Mother to Stockport Infirmary in his car. I'd travelled on trams, trolleybuses, charabancs and even Dad's coal wagon, but that was the first time I had ever been in a motor car.

Where the Halifax bank is now, on the corner of Bridge Street and Merseyway, was a provisions store called Nathaniel Gould's. At that time it was the best shop in town, but now it has a totally different appearance from what I remember from many years ago. Long before the precinct was even thought of, let alone built, and Lancashire Bridge stood in its entirety, the skyline of smoky old Stockport was completely different.

I remember going into Gould's many times to pick up groceries for Mum or Dad. I remember everything was sold loose. Sugar was weighed out and put into little blue bags, and you could buy whatever weight you wanted. Even if you wanted just a quarter of a pound, then so be it. They ground coffee in a grinder on the counter while you waited, and the smell was beautiful. I can still smell that shop today, a mixture of everything - bacon, coffee, cooked meats, all mixed together. I would hold back many times from getting served, just so I could be there a bit longer.

Butter was sold out of a wooden barrel stood on the counter. A few slats would be removed, and the shopkeeper would scoop out the butter. Using two paddles, he would knock it into shape, then wrap it in greaseproof paper for you. I was amazed at the knack he had of doing it so fast. Biscuits were sold out of glass-top biscuit tins, so you knew what was in them. Dried fruit, prunes and figs were stood in barrels on the shop floor, and people could help themselves. What a shop that was! I'll never forget it.

Going back up Great Egerton Street, I used to pass Corbishley's the pawn shop opposite the Three Tuns. I went in Corbishley's many a time to redeem Dad's ticket to get his suit out on a Monday.

I remember Ellis Sykes at the bottom of Prince's Street, full of weird and wonderful things. The only time I ever went into Ellis Sykes was to buy gas mantles, or a repair kit to fix the bucket or the tin bath if it had sprung a leak. The kit was two metal washers with a nut and bolt through them. You put a washer either side of the hole in the bucket, slid the nut and bolt through and tightened it up. It worked a treat.

On a Sunday, all the shops were closed except for the corner shop, which would open for just a few hours. What a relaxing, quiet day it was!

As we grow older, we console ourselves with the memories of our youth, as those are the times we cherish and remember well. Those memories are never forgotten, are held in our minds forever, and are recalled many times.

A SENSE OF COMMUNITY

Great Egerton Street looking towards Stuart Street. Harry Slacks is at the top of the steps.

Many is the time I look back thinking how we managed in the conditions of the slums of Stockport in the 1950s. But when you consider things, it really wasn't as bad as some saw it. I for one loved the slums. I didn't know anything else. It was cosy and everybody spoke to you. They shared what bit they had with you, and they'd lend you anything if they had it. They'd even give you their last crust of bread.

I was born in the midst of the smoky, black, crumbling, polluted mill town called Stockport. Soot-blackened smokestacks from the factories and cotton mills raked the skyline, each belching out clouds of obnoxious fumes and gases, adding to the pollution that killed many hundreds of

31

people. The polluted River Mersey also gave off its obnoxious odour as you walked along the old Mersey Way before the shopping centre was built.

On cold damp days, a thick blanket of this foul-smelling polluted air, called smog, would descend from above and darken the streets of Stockport. Visibility was so poor at times you could see no further than two paces in front of you. The smog was affectionately known as a 'pea souper' because it was thick and had a yellowish-green tinge to it. Black soot particles could be seen floating around in it, so covering the mouth was a must. We had to cover our mouths and noses with a scarf when we went out, and by the time we got to school or wherever we were going, the part where we drew breath through was covered in black slimy globules of soot.

I remember only too well walking the smog-filled streets over half a century ago. The year 1952 was the worst anybody had ever seen. The smog was the result of the huge number of coal-burning fires. That was the year it killed many thousands of people up and down the country. But it was also the turning point when the government decided to put an end to this environmental disaster by instigating the Clean Air Act.

This smoky old town caused many childhood ailments in those days, like coughs and respiratory problems, just as it did for adults. Death from respiratory disease was common then and the infant mortality rate was high. Many is the time I recall seeing tiny white coffins, not in a hearse as they were too expensive for many, but resting on the back parcel shelf of the local undertaker's car.

Stockport was bombed in 1940 but folklore has it that during the war Stockport got off pretty lightly from the

Luftwaffe. The reason was that they couldn't see us or the viaduct, which was one of their main targets, because of the pollution we created. Aerial photographs that were later retrieved were found to have a big black cloud of industrial pollution hiding Stockport from the air.

We were all guilty of doing our bit in adding to the pollution. Besides the coal, anything that would burn was always put on the fire to produce heat. Old worn-out shoes, bits of wood, paper, oilcloth and even vegetable peelings were used to back up the fire at night.

Now and again as we sat around the fire, clumps of soot would drop down and smoke would drift out into the room. Woe betide you if you were cooking something. This was a sure sign that the flue was becoming choked up and needed sweeping. But to employ a sweep in those days would cost around two shillings and sixpence, or half-a-crown as it was known by a few names. That was a week's rent for our house, a tad expensive and a messy job, so some people took to cleaning their own chimneys.

Chimney fires were a common sight in those days around Stocky, and seeing a chimney spewing out clouds of black smoke and red-hot soot particles was nothing unusual. The housewives would scurry about getting their clean washing off the lines before it got black.

Most of these fires were started inadvertently because the flue had not been cleaned for some time due to cost. But some folk would 'fire' them deliberately to save on the cost of a sweep. My dad did it too. I watched him stuff sheets of newspaper up the flue and light them. Then as the air started to draw, it took the burning paper up with it and subsequently set fire to the soot on its way up.

There were no telephones between our house and the fire station on Mersey Square. So once the chimney was alight, Dad would tell my brother to run to there. It was only about two to three hundred yards away, but by the time the fire brigade arrived from Mersey Square, the fire was roaring like a jet engine! Once they'd put it out, the flue was as clean as a whistle. A bit of a mess, but a few bob saved. I am sure the firemen knew it was deliberate.

I recall watching the gas lamp lighters with their long poles, cycling from one gas lamp to the next at night, lighting our way in the dim streets of Stockport. Although the lamps were bright, there were never enough of them. However, the streets we played on were as safe as playing in your own back yard. We kids were always safe playing on the streets in those days, even after dark. As long as our parents knew where we were, they never had to worry about us.

In those days, we could go out all day and leave the door unlocked, and even at night no one would come to any harm and no one would steal anything. They let kids play out alone, even in the early evenings on dark nights, knowing we were completely safe. They weren't perfect days, but we were happy. We had a great sense of security and safety, with a sense of belonging in the community. I think it sad that we no longer see kids playing in the street, playing the games that we once did. It's very sad indeed that the safety we then took so much for granted has, over time, been slowly eroded away.

In the solitude of the dark nights, I would make my way home from friends' houses. I'd walk alone along Newton's

Whim, a long and dark road that was as quiet as a graveyard. As eerie as it may have been, with the factory chimneys reaching into the dark sky like giant grave stones, the tall buildings looming way above me and the gas lamps casting their eerie glow into the mist of the cold night air, I never sensed any fear as I walked into the blackness ahead of me. All I could hear was the gentle hissing of the gas lamps as I passed by underneath them. I'd look down on the pavement and watch my shadow go before me as I walked under them. I loved the gas lamps. They had something about them and they were peaceful and serene. And when the mist was down, they gave off a light that was eerie, but soft.

Those of my age group will probably remember the 'knocker-up'. The knocker-up's job was to rouse the early-morning mill workers so they could get to work on time. The knocker-up would go from house to house, rattling a V-shaped wire on the end of a pole on the bedroom window and would not leave until they were sure the occupants of the house had woken up and answered.

We had one that came to our house, for sixpence a week. I always thought it was a man that did this job. Then one winter's morning, standing at the bedroom window looking out into the snow-covered courtyard with not a footprint to be seen in the blanket of pristine white snow, I saw a dark figure appear out of the ginnel. It was clearly a very large woman, well wrapped up against the cold blast of the winter's morning. The big boots she wore left a trail of dark prints behind her as she made her way across the yard to our house.

Raising her pole, she twisted it back and forth rapidly, so the v-shaped wires on the end of the pole rattled on the window.

Dad shouted, "Right!" to let her know he had heard and was awake, and back came the faint reply, "It's seven o'clock, Alf." Then away she went to her next call.

This was before alarm clocks were affordable or reliable. I don't ever recall seeing a clock in our house, but we didn't really need one. Life was never ruled by the clock. The radio was our timekeeper with the constant updates on the time. Or if the radio wasn't on, the periodic sound of the different factory hooters could be heard all over Stockport at clocking-on and clocking-off times, giving us the time of day.

On Sundays, the peal of bells from all the different churches around Stockport would also let you know what time it was. The sound of those church bells is one thing I miss, very much so today on a Sunday. Life was taken at a leisurely pace then, with no rushing about like we do now. Now it's no time to wait! No time for this, and no time for that. With all the hustle, bustle and stresses of modern-day life, we don't seem to have time for anything, or anyone, anymore.

It wasn't just the sights and sounds that would waft our way, it was the smells too. The courtyard where I lived was only yards from Hewitt's tripe dressers and Harry Slacks, the animal slaughterhouse on Stewart Street. Here, the sickly smell of rotting flesh and rendered fat and bone meal would linger all day. The stomach-churning smells from the slaughterhouse would cover most of the surrounding streets even up to St Mary's School, where on some of the worst days we were instructed to keep the windows closed.

And not twenty yards from our front door was Broad's stables, where the smell from the piles of musty rags collected by the rag-bone men, and the mountain of steaming horse manure, was a breath of fresh air compared to the putrid smell of Slacks. On warm summer nights, the smell of old damp clothes piled high in the yard drifted in the night air through our open bedroom window.

In a corner just the other side of the wall next to our row of toilets was the manure that was mucked out of the stables every day. It was piled high and left steaming for days, and the distinctive smell of horse manure and horses lingered over the courtyard day and night.

Joseph Broads, known as Broady's, ran the rag merchants on Great Egerton Street. They hired hand carts, and horse and carts, to the 'tatters', the rag and bone men, and these were usually hired by the day. I lived at the side of the stables, and every morning we'd see the tatters going out on their rounds for the day.

We used to love feeding the horses as they returned to Broads in the evening, and we'd save any stale bread to give them, and maybe the odd carrot. Strange how the horses always recognised us, as when they passed by they would walk over to us looking for their treats of bread or carrot.

As we lay in bed, we could hear the nags nattering to each other, and their hooves clattering on the granite cobbles. I remember the winter of 1953, which was a harsh winter with plenty of snow. The family was asleep in the dead of night when an almighty crash woke us all up. The snow had built up on the corrugated tin roof of the stable, and become too heavy for it, and the roof had given way under the strain. Luckily no horses were hurt that night.

Many tatters had their own call signs. Besides the familiar call of 'Raaag n booooone', some had a handbell or trumpet. I knew of one who used to rattle dinner plates together, that he later gave away. Or you could have a different-coloured donkey stone which he kept in an old rusty biscuit tin on the back of the cart. If Mother said she had enough stones, he would give us a balloon instead. It used to encourage us kids to mither for whatever old clothes we could muster together.

Times were hard, and I remember on occasions when Mother was short of money, she would put the old clothes in a suitcase for me to take them round to Broady's to weigh in. Old woolly jumpers used to fetch a good price. I remember sometimes coming back with around two bob to half crown, which would feed our family for the day. I think Joe was a little generous then.

I thought, till recently, that rag and bone men had all but disappeared. Not at all! In fact, there's more of them now than when I was a kid, only these days it's become a very lucrative commercialised industry with vans and loudspeakers two to three times a day. There are the plastic bags put through your door to fill and leave out for collection in the name of charities. They offer to donate £50 per ton collected to charity, when old clothes are fetching £1,000 plus per ton. How kind of them. What a racket it has become now!

HOMELY CONVERSATIONS

Bridgefield Street, looking west to the viaduct.

I will always remember the time I spent growing up in Old Stockport Town. All the family were still together, and the drug culture, crime rate and antisocial behaviour were non-existent. In my day 'hemp' was something produced in the local factories, and used in the making of textiles; 'grass' was the green stuff that we played on in the Red Rec; 'coke' was a soft drink, if you could afford one; and 'pot' was something your Mother cooked the 'tater 'ash' in.

In my mind's eye I can put all our neighbours' houses back where they once stood six decades ago. I remember the names of some of the residents that lived in Bridgefield and can put them all back in their respective homes. Walking along Great Egerton Street on warm summer days, I would see many of the elderly residents sat outside on chairs, whiling away the time of day and chatting over a cup of tea or a cigarette. Neighbours would have homely conversations over the garden fence or nip round to borrow a bob for the gas, a bit of milk, or a cup of sugar. Periodically, I would be asked to run to the corner shop for those not so sprightly on their feet, getting the odd penny or two to trade for sweets.

I would always find Mrs Rogers, a white-haired old lady who lived on Brown Street at the top of our ginnel, sat outside in her wicker chair, propped up with cushions. She would be surrounded by boxes of old brightly coloured coats, some of which were cut up into strips. With a square of hessian sacking on her knee, she would push the strips of cut-up coats through the hessian with a tool. She'd be making marvellous brightly coloured rugs to sell for a few bob to eke out her meagre pension. Mrs Rogers would sell them around the neighbourhood or make them a particular size or colour for customers. I would spend a little time sat on the doorstep alongside her, watching her make them. I would sit chatting to her many a time, and would watch in amazement at the lovely colourful designs she created from old cast-off clothes.

Mrs Rogers lived in a back-to-back just like ours, with one room up and one room down. She was too old to climb the stairs though, and only used the one downstairs room. Mrs Rogers would ask me to go inside and make a cup of tea for us both. As I walked into her neat downstairs room, I was greeted by a large cast-iron fire grate. A beautiful rug that she had made herself lay in front of the hearth. There was a neatly made bed in the corner and a highly polished dining table in the middle of the floor. It was covered with a lace tablecloth, and in the centre of the table was a beautiful green glass oil lamp that she used for lighting. I always remember how neat, clean and cosy the room looked. Such simple comforts made a house a home. I remember many a house around Bridgefield that was kept like that.

I'd make our cups of tea then go and sit on the doorstep in the warm sunshine alongside Mrs Rogers. She was a sweet old lady who had the time of day for anyone.

"Are you going to the shops, Arry? Could you get me two sausages, please?" There were no fridges in those days and perishables were bought on a daily basis. I would also be asked to fetch them some 'snuff' from the corner shop. Snuff was powdered tobacco and it was sold in little tins at fourpence a time. I'd often watch in amazement the oldies partake of one of the few pleasures they had in life. With their little snuff boxes, they'd take a pinch out, holding it between thumb and index finger, or place a bit on the back of the hand, and then sniff it up their noses. I never understood then why they did that, but who was I to question it? I always got the odd penny or so when asked to run to the corner shop to pick up their daily fix.

I can remember visiting lots of house-proud old dears, and Betty's house sticks in my mind, as it was the best-kept house I'd ever seen. Though the building was very old, inside was a different world. It was absolutely spotless. Betty was always cleaning and polishing, and as the door opened you could smell the Mansion House polish. I remember her always polishing the lino-covered floor, which was scattered with pristine and beautiful rugs. The cast-iron fire grate gleamed. A neatly made bed was in the corner and a small kitchen was just off the one room she had. There was no upstairs.

Beside the well-polished front door with its shiny brass finger plate, there was quite a long flight of stone steps that led down to Newton's Whim. These led into a yard on the Whim, where the toilet was, and the bins were kept. There was also a very large rusting old boiler which I think had been used by one of the first mills to use steam.

Next door to Betty on Stewart Street was a French polishers, Joe Ward. I'd call in to Joe's some days when I was off school and help him tidy up, because Joe was a very messy person, and his workshop was always untidy. I'd go around moving all the glass jam jars that had hard brushes and gone-off polish in them, and the pads he used for his work. He always made me welcome as I walked through the door. When time came for dinner, Joe would make a pint pot of tea for himself, and a small cup for me, and he would always give me one of the sandwiches he'd brought for his dinner.

Gertie was another old-timer and I'd often pass her house on Great Egerton Street. I can see old Gertie now, stood on the step as she usually did on nice days. Gertie was an invalid who had a bad leg so she couldn't do much for herself. I never liked going to Gertie's, as she always had us cleaning the wooden chair after the cat had weed on it, or that's what she told us. I knew different.

I remember Gertie very well. Mother sent us over to Gertie's in a morning, so she could watch us for an hour before going to school as Mother had to go to work. Mother worked at the Welkin Mill as a doffer. Gertie lived just where Red Rock stands now, about halfway down. Mother would send us across Great Egerton Street with a packet of cornflakes and a bottle of sterilized milk. As we sat round the table for our breakfast in

Gertie's living room, she put our cornflakes in dishes and then said, "Sorry, there's no milk. You'll have to put a drop of hot water on them." I never understood that as I'd just brought a full bottle over with me. She'd keep the milk for herself. Talk about robbing the poor.

When I look back now, some of it reads like a page torn out of a Charles Dickens novel. I remember the resident that lived in the back-to-back to us. Our house was in Robin Court, theirs was on Brown Street. Many of the residents would not venture out after dark to go to the outside toilets, mainly because of the rats, so they used the guzunder for the night. Just as we did. We'd take them over to the outside toilets to be emptied the following morning. But some of the residents, like the one at the back of us, were too bone idle to walk the distance. We heard, and saw on occasions, the sash windows slide up and the contents of the guzunder come hurtling through the open window and splosh onto the cobbles in the middle of Brown Street. To our relief, a few years later these neighbours moved up to Doris Road.

But worse was to come. An old spinster named Kitty moved in after they left. She did the same and used the guzunder at night, just like everyone else. However, she must have saved it up a few days then poured it down the kitchen sink, which was back-to-back with our drain. There was a large hole where the waste pipe went through the wall. The rising smell was evil! Would the last one out of the house please leave the door wide open? We stood shivering many times in the courtyard waiting for the house to clear. So, if you get a strange smell around Red Rock, you will know what it is and where it's coming from.

I remember one night, a bitterly cold winter night around January 1955, when I was walking home along Great Egerton Street. I'd just passed the old lodging house. The lodging house was an old bailing mill before being used as accommodation for tramps or homeless men. It was about four floors high but only the ground floor was used for the old geezers. I paused for a moment, as the door was open. Peering in, I saw many beds arranged down the sides of the old mill. A great big fire was burning in the centre on one side, and the fireplace was so huge they were burning full-sized orange boxes. I noticed that many of the old timers put the feet of the beds into their shoes. It seemed funny at the time and I used to wonder why someone would put a pair of shoes on a bed. I never understood until years later that it was to stop others from stealing their footwear.

That night, it was too cold to hang around, so I started back home up Great Egerton Street as it had begun snowing. I reached the school canteen on the corner of Newton's Whim when it started to come down really fast and heavy in large flakes. Before long I looked like a little snowman. I was just nearing the bakery, between Woodman Street and Brown Street, and I could see the faint glow of another fire through the blinding and driving snow. A few yards along, I could see it was a brazier. Workmen had started work on Egerton Street and a night watchman was on duty. As I passed, he was sat in his little sentry box looking all warm and snug.

"What are you doing out in this weather, at this time of night, sonny?" he said. "Come in for a few minutes and see if it eases off a bit. Where do you live?" I told him I just lived over the road.

"What's your name?"

"Arry," I said.

"Hello, Arry, I'm Joe." I sat down on his makeshift seat, two planks of wood on two piles of bricks. "I'm just about to make a cuppa. Do you want one?" A black cast-iron kettle sat steaming on the brazier with the lid bobbing up and down.

By now my legs were burning from the heat of the brazier so I shuffled back a bit away from the heat. I looked out onto Great Egerton Street and saw a Christmas card scene of driving snow, with a thick layer on the floor, and people walking to and from the Jolly Carter pub. I looked back to see Joe pouring the hot water into a brew can with two cups on the side. He even shared his sandwiches of boiled ham. The comfort and snugness of this job made up my mind that when I grew up, I was going to be a night watchman.

I remember every Saturday morning, one of the residents on Brown Street put on a Punch and Judy show for all the kids on the estate. I remember walking down the ginnel where he lived, to be met with rows of orange boxes in the courtyard, that he used for seating. He cut up apples and oranges and put them in a bowl of water for the kids to help themselves to during the show, and he charged every kid a ha'penny. It was very popular and there was a full house every week.

People used to look out for us kids in those days. They shared with us what little they had, whether time, food or attention.

BACK-TO-BACKS

Robin Court, where I used to live.

I can still see the streets as they used to be. I remember the quaint little cobbled courtyards. There were dozens of these little communal yards dotted around Bridgefield. I knew them all as I lived in one of them.

Our house was a dilapidated crumbling brick-built cube that bore no resemblance to the houses we know today. It was one of many hundreds that were built in the 1800 to 1840s by the cotton mill owners to accommodate the workforce brought in by the Industrial Revolution. They were cheap, quick to build and very small. The large families of the mill workers resided in them, many in cramped unsanitary conditions. By the fifties, the houses had been inhabited long past their use-by date. They were cold and damp, and had rotting window frames, rickety staircases, sagging walls, leaky guttering and broken bannister rails.

The houses on the estate around Bridgefield Street and Great Egerton Street were the old two-up two-down terraced type. Most of the houses of the time, from Brinksway to Portwood, and from Heaton Norris to Hillgate, consisted of terraced houses like this. However, some of the two-up two-down terraced houses that lined the cobbled streets of my hometown were divided into two living accommodations, having only one room up and one room down. These were known as 'back to backs'. We, a family of two adults and four kids, lived in one of these, in Robin Court. Another family, the Durrs, lived on Brown Street in the other half behind us. So that was two families, a total of eleven people, living in a small two-up two-down over-crowded terraced house. The rent that Mother paid was half a crown a week, two shillings and sixpence, or twelve and a half pence in today's money.

The houses were built of brick with slate pitched roofs, single internal walls and no cavities in the outside walls. Many had stone-flagged floors downstairs, covered with oilcloth. They afforded no such luxuries that we take so much for granted today. And our house was no different from any other on the Bridgefield estate. None had running hot water, central heating, bathroom or inside toilet.

Robin Court, where I lived, sided with Great Egerton Street and Stewart Street. We lived at number two. It was only accessible from the streets through narrow passageways, or covered ginnels, with barely enough room for two people to pass each other should they meet. In the blackness of the night, you had to walk slowly and feel your way along, holding out your hands to each side wall to steady yourself from falling over the uneven cobbles.

The one and only entrance door opened out into a courtyard facing a row of six brick-built, slate-roofed privies (toilets) which were shared by other residents of the yard. There were usually two households that shared a toilet. So a yard with twelve houses would have six toilets to share between them. Residents used to take it in turns on a weekly basis to keep their allocated toilet clean, and 'cream stoned' the inside and the outside step. I saw many an argument arise because someone had missed their turn cleaning, and not replaced the squares of newspaper hung on the nail behind the door.

I remember when we would step outside our house into the courtyard, on summer or winter evenings, and we would be met with the warm glow of light from the houses across the yard. The yellowish light from the small sash windows glowed on the cobbles. Many a time at night, I would see an oil lamp drifting across the yard, with the man of the household going to the loo with a paper tucked under his arm, maybe for a quiet read. Not many others would venture out after dark to cross the courtyards, for fear of rats. The courtyards were all unlit and care had to be taken crossing them. It was quite eerie at night to see washing left out, with white sheets and shirts flapping in the breeze. As a kid, when I walked across the courtyards at night, going home alone or to the outside lavvy, my imagination played havoc with me. I imagined all sorts of things lurking around the bottom of the passageway waiting to grab me, or ready to jump out of one of the privies as I passed by. Should anything have moved or made a sound on those nights I don't think I would have been here today. Should I go, or should I not? Maybe I'd wait till later and use the 'guzunder' instead. The guzunder was the chamber pot we all had in our bedrooms.

The slaughterhouse, which was only a few yards away from our house, attracted the rats. We would stand at the bedroom window at dusk, watching the rats scurrying around the courtyard, and maybe hear the odd scream now and again of some poor unfortunate female who had just encountered one while venturing over to the loo.

In summer we had to deal with all the smells that the heat brought out, but in winter the challenge was the cold. I always anticipated the arrival of snow, which often fell in those days. I would stand at the window watching it coming down, very heavy and in large flakes that covered the courtyard in a layer of white. By morning it was ankle-deep. On winter mornings, I'd look out of the front door only to see the courtyard covered in a blanket of snow. Grabbing one of the coats off the bed, that we used as extra blankets on those cold winter nights, I'd throw it round my shoulders. The large coat trailed on the floor as I made my way down the bare wooden staircase. I slid the door bolts back and opened the door. An icy blast rushed in. I'd then traipse across the courtyard in sub-zero temperatures to the outside lavvy.

The wind would often have driven the snow under the toilet door during the night. I often found that the oil lamp which hung on the stop tap, that used to keep the water pipe from freezing, had gone out during the night, and the pipes and cistern were now frozen solid. The lead pipe was swollen and had obviously burst although it was still frozen. That meant a trip down to Portwood for me later, to inform the local plumber, Mr Gandy, that we had a burst pipe, and would he come out and repair it.

Going back to the house, I would find Mother poking the ash out of the fire grate and opening the dampers to rekindle the still-smouldering fire that had been banked up the night before with slack. That meant another trot across the yard in the cold for me, to empty the ash pan in the dustbin that was kept in the bin shed. The bin shed was the old midden where kitchen, animal and human waste used to be tipped.

During the day, however, the yard would be a hive of activity: the housewives would be stoning the steps, hanging out the washing, or having a fag and a natter with their next-door neighbours. We'd often sit there too, watching the world go by.

I remember during thunderstorms, my sister and I would sit on the bottom stair looking out of the door across the courtyard. The cobbled yard had a blocked gully, and during heavy rain the yard would flood. Rain bounced in the great lake and me and my sister were mesmerised watching hundreds of bubbles appear and then pop. Mother said the door had to remain wide open just in case a thunderbolt was to hit us, as it had to have somewhere to get out. I perceived these thunderbolts to be great balls of fire. I'd sit on the stair keeping one eye on the outside watching the bubbles, and one eye on the fireplace waiting for this ball of fire to come rushing down the chimney and race across the living room and out of the door. Mother! The damage you did to me telling me that.

So that was life on Bridgefield. I still hear the voices and the laughter I was so used to when I lived there. It was a great life, but a bloody hard one. And I loved it.

ONE UP, ONE DOWN

Greens Place in the 1950s.

Sometimes, deep in thought, I take trips alone down memory lane. Wonderful memories start pouring back, remembering as we stepped into the house from school on those dark cold nights. None of the houses had inside bathrooms or running hot water or central heating, and many were still lit by gas, just as ours was. Heating was from a large black cast-iron fire grate in the living room. This was the focal point of family life in the home.

The fire I have now is nothing like the one we had then, how I wish it was. A big black monstrous thing, it towered way above me, but this monster was the heart of family life in those days, and every mother's pride and joy. It mesmerised me as it shimmered in the glow of the gaslight at night. The red-hot coals spitting out their bright yellow flames lit up the living room.

Mother would put on more coal and hold a sheet of newspaper over the grate with the help of a shovel, to draw the fire. As it roared back into life, the paper would begin to scorch in the middle and go brown. She knew then it was time to remove it before it burst into flames.

The gaslight would be turned off most of the time to save gas, and candles or night lights would be burning along the mantelpiece. As the fire flickered brightly in the grate, we'd turn around to see our shadows dancing eerily on the back wall and ceiling. We kids would sit around in the comfort of the emanating heat, laughing and giggling and playing our simple games of I-spy and hangman. There wasn't much else to do in the dark nights of winter. The winters seemed much harsher then and seemed to go on forever. Having no electric meant we had to read our books or comics, or play indoor games, by gaslight.

Dad would be asleep and snoring in the only armchair we had after a cold, hard, freezing day delivering coal around the cobbled streets.

Many homes in the centre of Stockport were built around 1840 to 1860, long before electricity became widely available. Our old house in Bridgefield didn't have electric. In this day and age, it does make me wonder sometimes how we used to get by without electricity, but everything worked fine then: we didn't need it and we really didn't have a use for it.

Gaslight was used to light the only room downstairs. Dad was a tall guy and many times he would lean over the table to get something and catch his head on the gas mantle. That meant no gaslight for the night, just candles and the light from the fire. It also meant another trip to Ellis Sykes on Prince's Street the following day to get another mantle. Gas mantles were very fragile and could not be touched once they had been burnt off. They needed renewing every few weeks or so as they used to wear out. The fabric would become thin and weak and the gas pressure alone would blow a hole in them rendering them useless. If the gas was running low, Mum would light a few candles and line them up on the mantelpiece to save gas for cooking and boiling water for tea. Many people only used oil lamps or candles for lighting. Ellis Sykes on Prince's Street was where most people would go with a container to get the weekly supply of lamp oil, which was paraffin.

One night the other week, when I was alone in the house, I turned the lights off and lit a few night lights along the mantel piece in my present home, just like Mother did in the old house. I sat in the dim light in the living room. The telly was off and everyone was out doing their own thing. The silence was deafening as I sat staring into the fire watching the yellow flames flickering around the coal. I was immediately transported back to the 1950s.

In our house we had gas for lighting but also for cooking. There was a small gas stove in the corner of the room. Mother would light the gas oven with a long wax taper or a coloured quill from the jam jar stood at the side of the cooker. Matches were expensive at thre'pence a box and were not wasted.

Some people weren't lucky enough to have gas to cook on. Those that didn't have gas used the open fire and side oven to cook with, even in summer. We had gas in our house but sometimes our mother would use the side oven to save on gas. I had many a 'tater ash' or stew cooked in the side oven, that took nearly all day to cook. When I was round at my mates' houses, I'd see the frying pan being used on the open fire to cook meals with, or a pan of stew or spuds cooking on the bars above the fire.

A chore that many housewives dreaded was black-leading the fire grate. I watched Mother many times pasting on the Zee-Brite with an old shoe brush, then buffing it up with a few old rags. Her hands were as black as the thing itself by the time she'd done.

The fire was used for everything: as well as boiling water and cooking, it was also used for drying clothes, even warming our socks and gloves before putting them on to go outside.

After playing on the dusty streets of this grimy, smoky town, I'd go home as black as the ace of spades. I'd then have a good tubbing in the old tin bath in front of the fire, and more than once I was stood in the dolly tub instead.

On a Sunday night, the tin bath would be brought in from outside and put in front of the fire. When not in use, it was always hung on a nail in the yard. Water would be heating in buckets on the open fire and on the gas hob cooker in the corner of the room. The little ones were always first, one at each end of the bath, bigger ones after. Adults were last, after we had gone to bed. The same water was used for all, just topped up with hot for the next one. The water was ladled out of the bath with buckets and poured down the sink when it was finished with. For those who had just washed their hair at bath time, the gas cooker oven was our hair dryer. We would stand or kneel in front of the open door drying our hair.

There was a brown stone slop sink wedged between the walls under the stairs at the highest point of the staircase. It stood on two brick pillars and a thick lead pipe with a tap on it was fastened to the wall. As you stood at the sink, the coal for the fire was stored behind you. I remember the musty smell that emanated from there as it was very damp. There was a hole in the wall where the lead pipe from the sink waste went through to the outside drain, and the smell was sometimes awful. Dad used to stand at that sink having a wash and shave, and it was also where we had a wash for school. I loved the smell of the soap we used, the red Lifebuoy on the shelf above.

The stairs from our one room on the ground floor led to our one upstairs room. We'd walk up the bare, wooden, creaky old staircase and, turning left at the top, there were the three beds. Our one and only bedroom had three beds in it - two singles and one double, with a narrow aisle between them about a foot wide around each bed. My two sisters were top-and-tailed in one single bed and myself and my brother slept in the other. We all slept peacefully underneath the few blankets we had, with the heaviest coats on top for extra warmth in winter.

There was just a lino floor, with no room for anything else. The room did not have wallpaper and was painted with 'distemper', a type of emulsion paint made by mixing pigments with water and a binder. There were very limited and basic colours, and ours was dark pink.

The bedroom was a draughty hole. I remember the window had small panes of glass in it. One of the panes was broken and covered with a piece of cardboard, but the wind still howled through it. When it rained, we had to catch the drips coming through the ceiling in buckets, but not the one we used for the 'guzunder'. The guzunder saved us many a trip across the courtyard on those cold dark winter nights.

The bedroom was always freezing cold. I remember we kids would take the hot shelves out of the fire grate oven downstairs and wrap them up in towels to put in our beds to warm them up. The oven was also used to heat bricks, and we'd wrap them in towels too and use them as foot warmers in bed. They had been in the oven all day and were quite hot. That was fine, and they kept our feet warm for about an hour, but once they went cold, we'd throw them on the floor. We'd take them down in the morning ready to heat up again for the next night.

After we got into bed, we'd soon snuggle down under the blankets. On cold frosty winter nights, we would shiver our way to sleep under the added weight of any available overcoats laid on top of the blankets. Occasionally we'd wake up shivering during the night and try to retrieve those that may have slid onto the floor or been nicked by the other occupant of the bed.

There was no light in the bedroom, neither gas nor electric. All we had was a little night light candle that stood in a saucer of water on the small mantelpiece. The little light it gave off was very dull, and made the room looked eerie and ghost-like. But when the fire was lit, we could see a little bit better, and we'd watch the shadows made by the flickering flames dance on the ceiling as we fell asleep. Really cold winter nights were the few occasions we were allowed a fire upstairs. Father would take a shovel of hot coals from the downstairs fire, carry it to the bedroom fire grate and stoke it up with fresh coal. The light from the fire was a bit dim but sufficient for us to see with.

There were no mattresses on the beds in those days, just what we called 'palliasses' or 'ticks'. It was many years later before I realised Mother was not calling them pollyasses. Palliasses were a large sack the size of the bed, made of strong, stiff material such as canvas, then filled with flock. Bolsters (double-sized pillows) were made the same way. I remember Mother would sit and unpick the stitching across one edge of the palliasse, then tip the flock onto the bedroom floor in a corner, and do the same with the bolsters. These were then taken to Bann Street wash house to be cleaned and dried before being refilled with the flock and sewn up again before night-time. I remember helping Mother to shovel the flock back into the palliasses and playing on the pile that was left waiting for the next fill.

Father was a bit strict at times, but that's what made us what we are today. Mother was the soft one, always giving in to us kids. I remember the times I got into trouble and would be sent to bed without any tea. There I'd be, feeling sorry for myself, sat on the edge of the bed with the steel bar beneath my knees. Sometimes the palliasses were a bit thin on the edges. I'd be staring into the cold fireplace, as the fire had long gone out. Once Dad had fallen asleep in his chair downstairs, I'd hear the stairs creaking and knew it was Mum sneaking up a few jam butties and a cup of tea. What a welcome feast that was! I loved dunking my jam butties in my tea and slurping the warmed-up jam from inside my butty. Better still, when it was toast there'd be all those black bits floating about in the greasy film on top.

I remember me and my siblings waking up on those terrible cold winter mornings. It would be nice and warm in bed, except for a cold nose. Peering over the top of the blankets towards the window, I would see the light of the new dawn breaking through the layer of ice on the inside of the windows, making it impossible to see out. We never dared to scrape it off for fear of the glass falling out of the rotting frames. One piece of glass was broken, and the corner was covered in a piece of cardboard to stop the snow and draught coming in.

Just as dawn was breaking, I'd sit up in bed. Mum was always up with the larks. Sometimes Mum would inadvertently wake me as she brushed past through the narrow gap between the beds. Bleary-eyed, I'd look around, but my sibs were usually still sleeping.

I'd catch a glimpse of Mum disappearing down the rickety wooden staircase to start breakfast. I knew, though, it was not seven o'clock as the knocker up had not yet been to our house. I'd get up, not disturbing Dad, and wander over to the window to see what the day was going to turn out like. I could hear the clogs of the early-rising mill workers clattering on the cobbles outside as they made their way to work in the grimy cotton mills of Stockport, clogs scraping and clattering on the pavements. Their hair would be tucked up in turbans, and strands of cotton clung to the clothes like it had just been snowing. Factory hooters sounded all over Stockport as they headed to the mills.

Even so, life in our 1950s house was bliss compared to the noisy environments we live in today. No washing machines, televisions or stereos would disturb the night air, and home life was pretty quiet, especially at night. Traffic noise was non-existent then and the sound of cars or motorbikes never existed in our back streets. All we could hear was the hissing of the gas lamp, the odd crackle from the fire maybe, or a bit of entertainment from the odd neighbour having a row a few doors away. That used to set the curtains twitching, and a few nosy women would innocently stand at their doors, earwigging. Sometimes I would see things thrown through windows when the housewife missed the hubby: cups and plates were a favourite, and even an alarm clock one morning landed in front of me on Brown Street. Mostly it was quiet and peaceful though.

Those days are now far away, yet they are so clear in my mind I remember them as if it were only last week. They are now consigned to books of history and to the memories of those of around my age who may remember those days living on the verge of poverty.

THE GREATEST GIFT A PARENT CAN GIVE

The Welkin Mill, where my mother worked.

My intention with these short stories is to recall some of the memories of how I, through the eyes of a child, perceived life in the slums of Old Stockport Town over six decades ago.

Mother was a 'doffer' at Welkin Mill in Portwood. Her job was to remove the full spindles or bobbins, and replace them with empty ones. I don't know how much they earned, but money was always tight. Like everyone else, they struggled to make ends meet from one Friday to the next.

My father was a coalman who worked for Morley's coal merchants on Wellington Road. Dad was actually our own coal man. We didn't have a cellar so the coal for the fire was stored under the stairs. Dad had to tramp through the living room to drop the coal. Sometimes there were great cobbers of coal (large pieces) and we had to break them up with a hammer. He used to put one or two of these very large pieces of coal in between the sacks out of sight on the wagon. With the help of yard staff and other drivers, he'd drive away with them. He never took anyone else's coal, and they all got the exact weight. This, incidentally, was always weighed again on the scales at the back of the lorry at the point of delivery, just in case any had dropped out of the open sacks.

The lorry he drove was an ERF, I think. It was old and draughty and had no heater. Dad would sit on the seat in between drops with a coal sack draped over his knees trying to keep warm. Now and again, he would lift the cowling cover a bit off the engine in the cab, which would blow a little heat in, but it was very noisy.

Sometimes Dad took me with him on deliveries. As we arrived at a drop, I would kneel up on the seat in the cab watching Dad through the back window. Dad would jump up onto the back of his lorry moving sacks of coal in readiness to deliver. Sometimes the coal in the sacks had turned white with snow in blizzard-like conditions. He'd jump down then start carrying those heavy sacks to the manhole covers on the pavements outside the houses. Some of the houses had cellars and he'd lift up these round cast-iron covers so as to tip the coal into the cellar below via the chute, then start dropping the bags in one by one.

I was sad sometimes when I would see him drop only one bag down into a cellar. Knowing this would be a hard winter, how long would that last the family? Some of the families I knew didn't have two pennies to rub together.

Our elders would spend their leisure time in one of the locals along the street: the Rock House Hotel, the Jolly Carter, or the Three Tuns on Great Egerton Street. The Jolly Carter was my parents' local. Dad liked his drink and on a Friday night he would go in there straight from work and not come out till closing time. My mother, fuming, would take Dad's tea over the road to the pub. It was all dried up and burnt with Mum trying to keep it warm in the oven for him. Mum would carry the hot plate with his tea on it across Great Egerton Street and plonk it on the bar in front of him, then walk away. Mother's actions caused Dad some embarrassment in front of his mates, and one hell of a row when he came home.

Mother was always working. I can often remember her standing over a bucket of water on the gas hob, or leaning over the kitchen sink under the stairs, washing a few small things by hand. The smell of soap powder and Lanry wafted through the room. Or maybe she was doing a bit of ironing on the dining room table. Now and then we could hear the heavy cast-iron clothes iron clanging on the gas hob as Mother put it back on to heat up. A woman's work was never done. Mum was always doing something: getting clothes ready for school, preparing meals for the next day, or sewing and darning. There was always something to do.

Mother was not only cook, cleaner, laundress and wage-earner in our house, she was also a nurse. Some of the remedies she used on us kids in those days would even make the local witch doctor cringe. When we got a boil or abscess, Mother would heat up a poultice of kaolin in a pan on the gas stove, smear it on a cloth and slap it on. Ouch! That was hot, but I loved the smell of the stuff, and it did do the trick.

If one of us got measles or chicken pox, Mother would put us all together to make sure we all got them at the same time, and we usually did. We'd then go to bed covered from top to toe in calamine lotion for a week.

Toothache was eased when Mother heated up a packet of Saxa table salt on the shovel over the open fire then wrapped it up in a clean cloth. We'd then put our face on it as we lay down and tried to go sleep.

Scrapes and grazes were covered in iodine, and we'd walk around with purple knees and elbows for days, looking like prats. Castor oil and cod liver oil were seemingly used to cure everything. Very rarely did we ever go to the doctor's surgery.

I remember my ailing grandma (my mother's mum) came to stay with us for a few months as she was not well enough to look after herself. Grandma slept in a bed downstairs. Living conditions for us were made even more difficult during that time. I remember Grandma Williams with great fondness. She used to send me daily to Meeson's sweet shop on Prince's Street for her Mint Imperials. I remember she always slept with a night light candle in a saucer of water at the side of her bed. I came home from school one day in 1955 and the bed was neatly made, but no sign of Gran. She had been taken into hospital.

A few days later, I had just been to Mrs Wild's shop on Great Egerton Street for a packet of biscuits for Mum. Me and my sibs were sat at the table eating them. The door was open and I saw a GPO post boy on his red bicycle slowly crossing the cobbled yard. He reached our house and handed Mother a telegram. The boy stood and waited in silence as Mum read it. After a couple of minutes Mother looked at the boy and said, "Thank you, young man. No reply." And off he went. Mum closed the door and drew the curtains together. We sat in silence, as we knew what had happened. Gran had passed away.

I am one of the many who were privileged to have been raised among a large, caring, hard-working community, and I'm supremely fortunate my parents gave me an upbringing that prepared me for the life most of us now live. They equipped me with the skills for survival and resilience. They gave me the greatest gift a parent can: the ability to cope in the face of adversity. We'd learn to make a pound do the job of a fiver, and a fiver last a week. I just wish I had realised what great gifts these were while my parents were still alive, so I could have thanked them. Our parents also taught us ethics and morals at a very young age, and you'd get a clip round the ear if you failed to abide by them.

I left school as thick as a plank, but I knew the Bible and the catechism from back to front. A fat lot of good that was in the real world of poverty, and I learned more after leaving school than I ever did there. But being so thick didn't stop me from becoming a successful businessman in later years. Being streetwise taught me how to make money. I carried that with me until I reached adulthood, then put it to good use. And I never forgot my parents in their advancing years, to repay them for all the love and affection they gave, often starving themselves to put food on the table for us kids. When I look back over my childhood, I wonder sometimes how we survived the harsh realities of living in the slums. But it was a motivator for me to never be as poor as our parents were. And it makes me appreciate the life I have now.

COOKING FROM SCRATCH

A cast-iron range like the one my mother used to cook on.

On those dark, cold winter mornings, as I looked over towards the bedroom window, that was by now iced up, I'd see the light of dawn just breaking through. I could hear Mother rattling the poker on the metal bars of the fire grate, clearing out the ash of the still-smouldering fire that had been slow-burning all night, trying to bring it back to life. I'd throw one of the coats from the bed over my shoulders and go down the creaking wooden staircase. I'd stand shivering on the hearth rug, waiting for Mum to get the fire going again.

Mother would then use the poker to drop the bars across the top of the open fire to put on a pan of porridge to cook while we got ready for school. While the porridge was cooking, Mum would start doing the toast. Piece by piece, it piled up on the plate on the table. The bread we used was from Mother Wild's shop on Great Egerton Street. It came in very long loaves wrapped up in white grease-proof paper. Much longer than the usual Champion or Mother's Pride, the bread was a bit smaller and thicker but had more slices. I seem to think now they may have been catering loaves. Other times, I'd see Mum frying bacon and egg above the red-hot coals of the fire. What a lovely smell that sent through the house. Proper bacon it was in those days, not pumped full of water to maximize profits like they do today.

During those cold winter days, the fire was on most of the day and Mum would cook the tea in the side oven to save on gas. It took an age to cook but was well worth it as the taste was very different to what you get from the processed rubbish we eat today. She would start cooking in the early morning as we got ready for school. We didn't have a kitchen, so she'd throw a corner of the tablecloth back into the middle of the table to start cutting up vegetables on the bare wooden surface. Then she'd put them into a brown earthenware pot and place it in the side oven. Once the shops were open, Mum would pop round to the local butcher, Evans Brothers on Prince's Street, for some minced meat to go with them. The smell of cooking drifted through the house all day.

After breakfast, on a weekday, we'd trek up the hill to St Mary's Roman Catholic School. Just past Corbishley's was the school canteen. Some schools did not cook on the premises but instead the dinners were cooked here on Great Egerton Street then delivered to the schools. What a wonderful smell we used to get when these ladies were cooking! Sometimes we would see the old guys from the lodging house stood at the canteen door asking for hand-outs, holding their plates and bowls. The meals were put into insulated aluminium containers, then onto those brown vans that delivered the meals to the schools. It was hot in that canteen and the cooks used to leave the doors open. We used to stand and watch them slaving away, cooking all those lovely meals.

We either loved them or loathed them, those school meals. I for one loved them. Friday was the best day for dinners, because we 'cat-licks' didn't eat meat on Fridays back then. The 'Proddy dogs' did, however. So we had fish and parsley sauce, or that lovely cheese pie I thought was the best. During the week, I remember we had minced meat pie and gravy, boiled spuds or mash, and veg. I used to sit waiting, with empty plate at the ready, for those lovely dinner ladies to call seconds, and on odd occasions even thirds. Yes, I'd go for thirds as well, if there was any. Mother always said I could eat one more potato than a pig.

Puddings, as I remember, were sago, sometimes with prunes, ladled out of those round insulated tubs. They looked a bit like frog spawn and were quite off-putting. Or there was semolina, which looked and tasted like baby sick. The rice pud was not too bad though. The best was the jam roly-poly and custard, or jam tart and custard. They were brill. They really stuck to your ribs (one of Mother's sayings), but they lay a bit heavy for the rest of afternoon. The only pudding I couldn't stand was blancmange. It was horrible stuff, and I'd rather eat my own vomit than that. But on the whole, they were well-cooked, wholesome meals, enjoyed by most school kids of the fifties.

When we came home after school on those dark, cold winter nights, we would open the front door and step into the dimly lit but warm living room, and the heat would hit us immediately. It was warm because the fire had been lit all day. The smell of Mum's cooking was amazing. Out of the cupboard would come a loaf of bread which Mum would cut up and put on a plate in the middle of the table. There was no butter, but if we were lucky there was a bottle of brown sauce.

Then a very large meat and potato pie in a hot earthenware dish came out of the oven, or a big brown pot with the stew and dumplings or 'tater pie in. Mum put it on the bread board then took out the plates that had been keeping warm on the top shelf of the oven. The hottest part of the oven was always on the bottom shelf as this was where the coals from the fire were put under. Mum dished the pie out onto the plates, then pulled out a roasting tin full of cooked sliced potatoes that were covered in water with a lid on, to stop them drying out. A pan of veg would be bubbling away on the gas cooker in the corner near the coal hole.

As Mum dished out the tea, she would put Dad's back in the oven to keep hot as he always called at the Jolly Carter on Great Egerton Street for a pint on the way home. A big pot of tea was always sat on the hob keeping warm, as Father always liked his tea strong and stewed. Other times, Dad would be already sleeping in the one chair in front of the fire. Mum would wake him saying, "Tea's ready, Alf." Dad was always served first.

During the week, dinner was maybe a tin of corned beef, turned into a corned beef hash. Or we might have a tin of spam, sliced and fried with chips or whatever else was going at the time. With a pound of mince and a few veg, Mother worked her magic like she always did. By adding a few carrots and onions, she made a stew with the mince, and served it with a pan of mashed potatoes, and cabbage or peas as a veg.

Sausages were mostly fried, served up with mash. Mother always put a great lump of Echo margarine in with the mash and a bit of sterra milk to mash it up to a cream. Mum didn't have a spud masher, so she used a Cheshire sterilised milk bottle she kept for that purpose. Once Mother had dished out the sausage and mash, she would pour the 'dip' the sausages were fried in over the mash. Or maybe she'd do a sausage casserole with an onion and all the other magical ingredients she added to make such perfect meals.

Stewing steak would make the perfect meat 'n' potato pie with a big thick crust. Just as it came out of the oven and was left to cool, Mother would send me to the back door of the UCP on Bridgefield Street for a bob's worth of chips to go with it. Or she'd maybe make a stew and fill the entire top of the pot with dumplings. With a few boiled potatoes, this made the most perfect meal, and I can still remember the taste today.

Liver, fried with an onion, was one of my Dad's favourite meals. Even today, if I'm cooking liver or bacon, I dip a slice of bread in the pan while waiting for it to finish cooking. I remember as a kid eating bacon dip butties, and I still relish the odd bacon dip butty even today. The aroma from Mother's cooking would waft all over the courtyard, and as we walked down the ginnel and through the front door on those cold winter days, it was amazing.

Friday night was always the chippy night and the two chippies, Hallats and Townleys on Bridgefield Street, were always busy. Chips were thre'pence and cod ten-pence, or you could have a silver hake at one shilling and a penny. I can still see the prices painted on the range mirror in whitening. I loved watching the speed Mary put those spuds under the hand chipper at the end of the counter. It was amazing but many a time I expected her to chip a finger or two. The perfect and traditional fat for frying both the fish and the chips is beef dripping or lard. Both give a crisper and tastier chip and fish batter. What ever happened to the traditional British chippy? Sadly, gone are the days of the fish supper (that's what we called them) wrapped up in newspaper with mushy peas and that lovely chippy sauce, or maybe a nice steak and kidney pud in a pudding basin. There are still a fair number of chip shops around, but they all seem to shut quite early on in the evening, well before pub closing time, at around 10 pm.

A handful of rice and a bottle of sterilized milk ended up as a nicely baked creamy rice pud for afters, done in the oven in one of those brown earthenware dishes. Or if Mother had kept any stale bread, she would make bread and butter pudding. By adding a few raisins and a little cinnamon she would turn it into a college pudding, perfect with custard. Or there were bananas sliced up into a bowl, with a sprinkle of sugar and milk on.

Chestnuts were a favourite snack of mine. I remember when chestnuts were available on the market and me and my sister would go up there to get a large bag. At night we would all sit on our little stools or kneel on the rug around a blazing fire to roast them. We'd line them up on the flat bars of the coal fire or put a few on the shovel, placing the shovel on top of the fire to roast them. We waited in anticipation for them to cook, but they still made us jump as they popped and flipped into the tin hearth below. Hot roasted chestnuts on any cold night were delicious.

And those pobs, bits of bread broken up in a cup with hot milk and sugar added, we virtually lived on those as kids. We had them for regular snacks and if there was nothing else in to eat, we were given just them.

On other nights, we'd sit in front of the fire with the toasting fork doing our suppers, and the smell of toast would then start filling the room. Most of the shops sold bread uncut till the early 50s, until sliced then became very popular. Mum would cut the loaves into slices which she'd pile together on the hob ready to toast on the end of the toasting fork. Once done, they were put on the table on a large dinner plate for us kids to help ourselves. I always dived in first for the crust. They were soft inside, crusty on the outside, and scrumptious with plenty of marg melting into the hot toast.

Once a piece of toast was done, we'd hand it to one of my siblings to butter it themselves. We never had butter only marg. We then had a choice as to what to put on our toast: jam, dripping or just marg. Echo margarine was not very nice, and Summer County margarine was the nearest we ever got to butter.

If you preferred, you could have dripping on your toast, with a pinch of salt. The dripping was always saved from the previous Sunday roast, then poured into a cup to be used during the week on hot toast. I couldn't wait to dig to the bottom of the cup to get at the jelly and the residue of the roast. Larvely jubbly!

Mum, however, used most of the dripping to make the gravy for the Sunday dinner. I remember how beautiful that gravy was. I even save the Sunday roast dripping today. I'd watch Mum make the gravy on Sundays for the dinner. She'd put the roasting tin on the gas hob then she'd mix the flour with the dripping and pour in the water off the spuds, add the browning, then cook it out. That gravy really made our Sunday dinner, and we always spent time mopping up the gravy with bread. I still do the gravy today exactly like Mother did. Those that join us on Sunday for dinner don't know how I make it, but I still get complimented on it.

As us kids lay in bed on a Sunday morning, I could smell the dinner cooking as Mother prepared it. What a smell that was, and our best meal of the week. It was breast of lamb, a cheap cut but loved by all the family especially with the roast spuds and dollops of mash. Mother cooked the lamb to perfection, crispy on the outside but soft and stringy on the inside. We kids loved it, and I still buy it sometimes even these days.

Us kids used to have treats sometimes too, but buying an ice cream in the 1950s was not as simple as it is now. Most shops didn't even have fridges, let alone deep freezers. We used to listen and wait for Simon on his trike, a three-wheeled bicycle that had a large, insulated box on the front. Simon was a chubby little man with a ruddy complexion who wore a white coat and cap and peddled his trike down Great Egerton Street, stopping periodically to ring a handbell. A cornet was tuppence, and a wafer a thre'pence, and there wasn't a great choice in those days, just one flavour and no ice lollies. But they were very welcome on a hot day, if you had any money. On top of the box where Simon kept his bell was a jug that he put this ice cream scoop in after each use. Any bits left on the scoop would then melt into the jug, and if we had no money, he would give us the jug to drink the melted ice cream from. Lovely jubbly!

The war years' food rationing had placed a considerable strain on the beleaguered housewife. In 1951, meat was still on ration, and there were still very meagre quantities, with the exception of horse meat. Horse meat was in big demand in those days as there were 'no coupons needed' and it was very cheap. I remember the horse meat shop on Great Egerton Street having a sign in the window that read 'This meat is fit for human consumption'. I went there many times to get 'steak' for Dad's tea. No doubt Mother may have put some to good use for us kids without ever telling us. I shall never know the answer to that. I also remember Dad sending me to the UCP shop many times for elder, tripe, chitterlings, savoury ducks and cow heel. How I remember looking in that window at some of the seemingly gruesome, unappetising things that lay there. Honeycomb tripe loaded with salt and vinegar was my Mum and Dad's favourite dish.

The healthy-eating brigade would have a fit now at some of the things we ate as kids. But what harm did it do us? None at all, and an overweight kid was rarely ever seen. Any extra calories we ate were always burnt off with the exercise we got. Also, all our meals were prepared and cooked from scratch, from the basic ingredients. There were no ready meals or frozen stuff then. Food tasted so much better, and we knew what was put in it. What a wonderful life we had as kids. I am thankful for all those years and all the 'bad things' that we used to eat and do, but it is why we are who we are today.

I came from a family of four kids in the fifties, and two more arrived in the sixties. I know how hard our parents worked to make ends meet and to keep us clothed and fed. In the fifties, money was always tight, but our mothers had that knack of making £1 do the job of £2. When I think back, I remember how Mother could muster a meal together with the minimum of effort and ingredients. Many a time at the weekends, Mother sent me to Brines Butchers on Underbank just before closing time, for a half-crown wrap-up. For that you would get some scrag end (neck-end of lamb), a bit of lamb's liver, a handful of mince, a bit of stewing steak, a few sausages or anything that had been left on the trays at the end of the day. You just took potluck what you were given.

All our mums knew how to cook in those days. Cookery in Britain during and after the war lacked variety and failed to inspire the palette, but the nation's housewives kept coming up with innovative recipe ideas for the limited range of available foods. As the old adage goes 'It's not like Mother used to make'. And never a truer word spoken. Our mothers had that instinctive aptitude to make many different tasty meals with the same basic ingredients. We seem to have lost the ability to do that these days, with all the ready meals full of junk. Many people have lost interest in cooking altogether. I have tried on many occasions to emulate mother's cooking, but those dumplings have always eluded me: they were something only she knew how to make so perfectly.

I have watched the changing face of my hometown for the last sixty years. But Stockport is nothing like how I remember it. Now it is just a shadow of its former self, compared to how I knew it as a kid. When I look up and down the back streets of Prince's Street today, I see the shadows of my distant past, a past where the poverty we endured left many deep-rooted memories. Some memories of the time I spent in the slums, I remember with great fondness. And some, even time will not let me forget.

TIMES WERE HARD, MONEY WAS TIGHT

Corbishley's pawn shop on the corner of Great Egerton Street and Hatton Street.

Whenever I think of those times, I remember the feeling of comfort and safety in the family home I once lived in. Even though I lived in a slum dwelling, I grew up surrounded by the warmth of a loving family, and a hardworking, strict community. We were poor, but we didn't know we were poor because everybody was the same. I loved the place I spent my childhood in, but I have no wish to return to the dark days and the terrible conditions of the 1940s and 1950s.

Times were hard and money was tight. I remember times in our house when the situation seemed hopeless. Mother did her best to look after us and put food on the table, but there was no generous benefits system like there is now. If you didn't work, you had no money, simple as that. Being 'on the NAB' (National Assistance Board) carried a stigma with it in those days. Most people were too proud to go asking for state handouts, but in some cases, they had no choice. Either that or go hungry, not like today when they take benefits as a right. Many of those hard-working people felt shame when they came out of work and had no choice but to ask for state handouts.

Everything was means-tested then. I remember the well-dressed man carrying a briefcase, who was from the NAB, calling at our house when Dad was out of work on very rare occasions. He would look around the house to see if we had anything worth selling to raise money before he would sanction any handouts for us. Woe betide me if I mentioned the radio wrapped up in the coal sack hidden at the back of the coal hole. It was the only thing we had that may have been worth a couple of bob. That was one place they never searched - they wouldn't have wanted to get their hands or suits dirty rooting in a place full of coal dust. The NAB would only pay out for the kids and housewife though. The fathers had to go and look after themselves, with relatives, or at the workhouse maybe.

Poverty was rife on the estate, more so for those with the larger families. Yes, I knew poverty; we became very close when we were kids. I remember the times when Mother didn't have two ha'pennies to rub together to look after four of us.

Walking around with holes in our shoes, I remember us traipsing along Underbank and up Hillgate to Gran's house on Canal Street for something to eat, then Mother taking us up to Hall Street and the National Assistance Board and threatening to leave us on the counter there.

I remember the rent was two shillings and sixpence a week, or half a crown. Many a time when the rent man called, Mother would tell me to get it off the table with the rent book and pass it to him. Even then, half a crown was a lot of money.

Friday night was 'tallyman' night. Everybody had a tallyman who collected instalments for goods paid on hire purchase. Some tallymen would get paid and some would get 'bumped' (not paid or missed). The loan man and the tallyman on a Friday night would be the first casualties when money was short, and they would get the silent treatment when knocking on the door. As soon as Mother caught a glimpse of the tallyman walking over the courtyard with his big black book in hand, we would be told to sit on the stairs and not make a sound. Mother would then keep watch through the net curtains until he gave up knocking and went away. Other times, it was me who got the job of answering the door while Mother hid behind it, and of telling them that Mam wasn't in. One of them craftily caught me out one night and said, "Ask your Mum if it will be alright to call tomorrow." I popped my head round the door and only got as far as saying, "He said will..." My ear was red for days after that, but not as red as my Mother's face was. We may not have been thankful then for the thick ears we got from our parents. However, we are forever grateful to them for blessing us with the knowledge and skills to deal with whatever life throws at us now they are no longer around.

I was always a bit streetwise, but as a kid you had to be to survive. Earning a few bob was not easy, but not too difficult if you knew how. This little rascal could charm the saddle off a nightmare at times. Getting freebies was no problem. Pollitt's potato merchants was on the corner of Bridgefield Street and the A6, Wellington Road. Many a time, I would call in asking if they had any 'faded apples'. These were slightly bruised and maybe needed a little piece cutting out. As I walked through the front door and stepped onto the bare, well-worn floorboards, I would see Harold loading the wagon out the back in the yard. Harold did the deliveries to the shops and chippies around the Bridgefield estate. Directly in front of me was the office. I could see behind the glass a little old lady sat on a stool beside George, and I took this to be his mother. George would come out and without saying a word go over to get a couple of apples which he'd saved for the kids on the estate. They were kept in a little basket above the potato hopper. On the odd occasion, an over-ripe banana might be among them. He'd take out a pen knife from his waistcoat pocket and cut out the bruised bits for us.

On my way home, I would call at Lowes the bakers on Prince's Street to see if they had any broken cakes. Nearly every time, I'd walk out with a couple in a bag, no charge. Those vanillas were unforgettable. Woods Florist on the corner of Woodman Street and Prince's Street was the same, only I'd look through the window to see if any fruit had been put in the basket at the side of the till. If any had been, we just had to go in and ask for it.

I would also slip down the ginnel at the side of Woollies and Marks and Spencer's. Round the back there was often a trolley with cakes and loaves of bread on it. I don't know whether they had been put out as rubbish or were awaiting collection, but I made their load a little lighter, and I'd whizz up Prince's Street with a bag full.

Life was hard and it was grim living in the vermin-infested terraced houses. Rats, mice, cockroaches, blackjacks, silverfish and bed bugs - everyone had them and not a day would go by without seeing one or the other. I remember Dad sat down for his tea one night and put his butties on a plate on the floor at the side of his armchair. On reaching down to pick up a butty, he spotted a mouse running back to its little mousehole at the side of the fireplace. Looking at the bread on his plate, he found a large piece missing as it was in the mouth of the mouse struggling to get back home with it. I remember Dad saying, "You're a cheeky little sod, but just for your cheek you can have it." Then he helped the mouse along by pushing the bread into the entrance to the mousehole, and I watched for about two minutes as the mouse pulled it in.

The bed bugs were the worst, and it was really difficult to keep them under control. This was not because the house was dirty, because it certainly wasn't. Mother was always cleaning, although it never looked any better once she'd done it. No, it was because of the poor state of the building. The bed bugs came out at night to feed on us, and we could see the red spots in the morning where they had been. No matter what Mum did, it was very difficult to get rid of them. Silverfish by the thousands also came out at night when it was dark and quiet.

All those sayings that Grandma said to us had their origins, and some derived from her younger days. One you might commonly hear today was 'Sleep tight and watch the bugs don't bite'. Well, in those days the little sods actually did. One occasion I remember was when Dad came home early one afternoon from his coal round and found Mother making the beds and cleaning the bedroom.

"What are you up to?" he asked.

"I'm putting these ladybirds out onto the bedroom windowsill," she said.

"Mary!" he gasped. "They are NOT ladybirds." Well, the look of shock and horror on my mother's face when he told her what they were, I can still picture today.

Leading to the lowest point under the staircase was the coal hole, where we kept the coal, along with the 'blackjacks'. One incident I remember well with those horrible things is when I put on my little wellies one morning to go across the courtyard to the outside loo. As I sat there, I began to feel something wriggling around my toes. Putting my hand in, I pulled out one of the biggest blackjacks I'd ever seen. The welly went in one direction, the blackjack in another, and I never did wear those wellies ever again. To this day, I am convinced it was this incident that created the morbid fear I now have of anything with more than four legs.

On warm summer days, large black flies that originated from the local refuse tip at Lanky Hill used to swarm over, attracted by the stomach-churning smell that emanated from Harry Slack's slaughterhouse on Stewart Street. Those flies that avoided a sticky end on the fly paper that hung down from the ceiling, were brought down in mid-flight by Mother wielding a pump-action spray tin of Flit (which was DDT). Any stragglers were caught in the clutches of Herbert, our huge resident house spider that resided behind the curtain in a large web.

Even though our house was damp and rotten in places, it was a place that I loved very much and can remember with great fondness and affection. All the childhood memories I hold were formed when I roamed and played in the back streets of Old Stockport Town. They are now all in the past, but they are not forgotten. The distant memories of the childhood I spent growing up in the slums of this old mill town seem as though it was only yesterday.

MARKET DAY

Stockport Market, 1948.

There are a thousand memories of Stockport market, each frozen in time, in such a small space, far too many to mention. They are now all in the distant past, but as long as I live they will never be forgotten. Stockport marketplace holds many special memories for me. In the fifties and through to the seventies it was a wonderful place.

The market kept me in a bit of spending money that my parents could never afford to give me. It also put many a cheap meal on our table. It was so busy and full of life, bustling with crowds of people, you could hardly move on a market day. You only have to look at some of the old photographs to realise what a fabulous town and marketplace we had then.

In my young days, I'd go shopping on the market with my mother. The atmosphere created by the bustling crowds and stallholders calling their wares and prices was something that could never be captured on a photo. Those market traders were the salt of the earth and they made Stockport market what it was. I remember on dark winter nights, the place used to be lit up brightly with those huge light bulbs that hung from the stalls, and the stalls were placed end to end as far as the eye could see through the bustling crowds.

The outside market was open two days a week, Fridays and Saturdays, and was open till late evening on Fridays to catch the mill workers on their way home with their pay packets in pockets. There were no supermarkets then and the local corner shops were expensive in comparison to the market, so everybody shopped on there to save a copper or two.

I loved exploring the market area but the one place I could never venture into was the indoor Hen Market. The smell used to make me feel sick, so I always waited outside for my mum. Over six decades later, I still remember that awful repugnant smell. And I can still see the blood-covered chickens hung up, the wet dead fish and the smelly cheese as though it was only yesterday.

When I was around eight years old, I had a Friday job on the market helping out on one of the stalls. I'd be up at six in the morning and on the market for about seven. I used to help the bag man just outside Dewhursts butchers with the shopping bags he sold, unloading his van and setting up his stall for the day's trading. Then around eight-thirty, he would send me to what is now the Staircase cafe for his usual jug of hot tea. I got ten bob for all that, then I'd dash off and leg it up Red Brow to school at St Mary's on Dodge Hill. I'd just about make it in time for assembly.

I'd go back to the market after school again and help to load the bag man's van back up at the end of the day. It was a long day for a young kid. Saturday was the same routine, but in between the loading and unloading I was not needed. So I used to go round the market collecting wooden orange boxes and tomato boxes to break up for firewood. I would break them up into large pieces and stack them into one large orange box which I dragged through Stockport all the way home. I bumped it down Dutton's Steps, then along Underbank, along Union Road, across Mersey Way and into Prince's Street. I stored the boxes in our bin shed across the courtyard, where I could keep my eye on them from our window. Then I'd go back to the market for some more.

Sunday morning was the time I'd spend breaking the boxes up into smaller pieces and bundling them up for firewood. I tied them up with bits of string I found on the market. I used to work at this in Newton's Whim, just across Brown Street. There were no houses on the Whim, so I never disturbed any residents. I'd then go selling the bundles around the Bridgefield estate. Everyone had coal fires then and firewood was always in demand for lighting the fire with. I did a roaring trade selling it at tuppence a bundle. And I delivered it to the door.

On Friday and Saturday nights after the market had closed, I paired up with a girl called Edna from Hillgate. We would go rooting through the rubbish that had been turned out of the veg stalls. During the course of the day, many stallholders dropped the odd penny, thre'penny bit or even a tanner among the apples or spuds when they were passed over to the customer. The stall holders often forgot to retrieve the coins at the close of business. Edna and I kept a sharp lookout for them and made a small fortune, which we would share out at the end of the evening. As the old adage goes, 'What the eyes don't see, the heart don't grieve.'

And as the darkening sky rolled in, we would search through the rubbish that lay on the floor waiting to be removed by the council binmen. We'd also look for vegetables that had been dropped or turfed out. Luckily there were plenty of them. As we rooted through, I'd pick up the odd apple, orange, spud or stray bunch of horse radishes. Most of these were fresh and still good to eat after I'd tarted them up a bit and taken any bad or withered leaves off. Some may have been slightly bruised, but if you cut out the bruises they were perfectly good enough to eat, just not to sell. Cabbage leaves, and cauliflowers that may not have been quite as white as people wanted, were all thrown out. Brilliant was the day when me and my sister would find a couple of pomegranates. We loved them. We'd cut them in half to share with our other sibs, and sit for ages with a needle each, picking out the juicy seeds at night in front of the roaring fire.

We were joined on the market by old-age pensioners, grey-haired and wrinkled, shawls around their shoulders, long black skirts stopping short just above their clogged feet, and shopping bags in hand. Sometimes younger women would come with kids in prams, and sometimes it was just kids on their own, kids with dirty faces and runny noses. They would sift through the mounds of rubbish, periodically picking up the odd potato, carrot or apple that had been dropped during the course of the day. This was a sight that made me very sad. I knew we didn't have much, but I was sure these poor souls had even less. I myself was doing it for the money.

Later on, I'd get a tomato box and fasten it around my neck with a piece of string (just like the ice cream lady's tray at the pictures) and go door-to-door selling my wares. The most I made in one night was six shillings. Over the weekend I made a bob or two for the gas meter maybe, a couple of bob for myself and the rest went in Mother's purse to buy a tin of corned beef or a tin of steak to make a few meals during the week. Sixpence was a lot of money in those days, and well worth the trouble considering the rent on our one-up one-down house was only two shillings and sixpence a week.

The things we used to think of to make that bit of extra cash! I can remember a few others, but a lot of kids had their own inventive ways. Some liked collecting any empty bottles that were left lying around: for milk bottles you'd get a penny each, mineral bottles were three pence, beer bottles were about two, but you had to be careful where you took them back to, as some off-licences only sold particular brands. If you ever came across a Soda Stream bottle, wow, you were in the money! There were three shillings on those.

Money was always tight with our parents, and we were never given any pocket money for spends. But now and again Mother would give us the odd shilling to go to the Plaza matinée on a Saturday afternoon. Other than that, we had to earn our own spends by running errands or taking empties back for a few sweets.

One thing we all remember as we get older is our childhood. And I for one had a good memorable childhood, a childhood I would not change for the world. I would not have had it any other way. We had nothing, but I never recall ever wanting for anything. We were poor, but we didn't know we were poor because everybody was the same.

YOU COULD NEVER WAG A DAY OFF

St Mary's RC Primary School, Dodge Hill. I am on the
back row, third from the right.

Life always looked rosy when I was a kid living on the
Bridgefield estate in the 1950s. But then, I keep a pair of those
proverbial rose-tinted specs in my top drawer, and now and
again I take them out and look at the life I spent in the slums of
Old Stockport Town as a kid. The derelict houses and boarded
up buildings with their crumbling brickwork and decaying
timbers were our playground. I clearly remember the wonderful

world of the childhood I spent roaming and playing on the dusty streets of this smoky old cotton mill town.

But when I take the specs off, I see the realities of what life was really like then. We always seem to recall the best bits of our childhood and it's the happy times we always seem to remember the most. But they weren't all warm sunny days spent playing out with our friends. In fact, we spent many days inside in our classrooms.

I attended just one school for the whole of my childhood. It was St Mary's Roman Catholic School on Dodge Hill. I remember the first day I started. I was just under five years old and I certainly didn't want to go that day. I still remember quite clearly Mother pulling me up the steps on Brown Street, then along Stewart Street, up the Rec Brow and into the infants school. I was dragged kicking and screaming all the way there. In my mind, even now, I can still hear those screams. Trying to get away from Mother, what a little sod I must have been for her. I was then pulled into the classroom by Miss Flannery, still kicking up a fuss. As she bent down to console me, I unintentionally punched her on the nose, and it turned quite bloody. After composing herself and holding a tissue to her nose, she sat me down in the sand pit that they had in the classroom. I was quite happy there for the rest of the day and not another sound was heard from me. If this was school days, it didn't seem all that bad.

At morning break, they came round with the school milk. I always remember those little bottles of milk we got. They were brought into the classroom part-frozen on those freezing cold winter days and were lined up on the heating pipes to warm up a little. On the days there were no deliveries, because of the severe weather conditions, we were given milk tablets instead. Not everyone liked them, but I loved them, and would go around at playtime collecting them off the kids that didn't want theirs. I'd go home with my pockets full.

I remember coming out into the little communal hall at that first dinner time, to find that the tables had been put up by the caretaker. I could smell the food as the dinner ladies got it ready for us. I remember it was sausage and boiled potatoes on my first day. I stayed for free school dinners and, as I recall, they were always delicious. As kids, we either loathed them or loved them, and whether they were free or you paid for them we all got the same.

The only problem I had with school dinners was when I got home there'd be a dinner waiting for us: a big pot of stew with big fluffy dumplings, or a tater pie in the oven in one of those big brown earthenware pots with a thick crust on top, or a big pan of tater' ash on the gas hob. We always found somewhere to put it though.

Those kids that had free dinners also got them during the school holidays, but we had to go to Christ Church dinner hall for them. I went to St Mary's School and always wondered what Miss Ledwich thought of that, us 'left-footers' going into a Protestant school.

The large main hall where we had our dinner at St Mary's was also used as the assembly hall and gym. The stage was part of the 'top girls' class whose teacher was Mrs Cassidy, the wife of Pop Cassidy, the headteacher. Under the stage was the cinema where films were shown, and the lads' weekly club was held. I remember the Christmas nativity play being carried out on that stage. On the hall floor, I can remember us boys with two left feet learning to dance. I hated that. 'The Dashing White Sargent', and the 'Veleta', how awful!

Who remembers those other embarrassing moments we had at school? First there were those medical examinations, where we all stood with virtually nothing on in front of our classmates while the doc checked every nook and cranny. Nuff said about that. Then she snapped in half what looked like a lolly stick and shoved it down your throat. It made me heave.

That did me untold psychological damage as to this day I can't even stand a lolly stick near me. Even if I see one on the floor I cringe and shudder at the thought, as it brings back such bad memories.

Then there was Nitty Nora the Bug Explorer, or the nit nurse. We'd queue up in a line in the classroom and move in one by one for her to rummage through our hair. We always watched to see who got the envelope. Now that was embarrassing, when she gave you an envelope to take home to your mum as it indicated to your classmates that you'd got nits. We got ragged for days after. "Don't go near him. He's got nits."

I remember that awful stuff they used, Sulio, that horrible yellow shampoo stuff. The smell of that alone should have been enough to kill them, and if you got it in your eyes you screamed blue murder and were left traumatised for a week after. Then out came that fine-toothed steel nit comb to dislodge the eggs. It's a wonder you had any hair left for the little blighters to hide in after that.

Then came the eye test, and they tried to get you to wear those NHS specs. Wire frames with sterilised milk bottle bottoms for lenses. "Sorry, mate, not a cat in hell's chance." I'd rather go blind first.

Then there was the school board's truant officer, a trilby-hatted guy in a mac, who'd come knocking on your door to see why you weren't at school. He used to frighten the life out of us kids. The times I used to dodge that guy! You could never wag a day off school as your parents always knew about it when he came round looking for you.

I spent all my weekdays at St Mary's school, and spent many Sunday mornings at the church as well. I remember the priest coming to our house in Robin Court, just a stone's throw from the church. Although we kids were in bed at the time he called, I was listening at the top of the wooden staircase. Everything was a bit cramped then, so nothing was missed and we could always hear Mum and Dad talking downstairs. I heard the priest say that I had not been baptised yet, even though I was seven years old, and he was questioning why. Arrangements were made for the following week. I remember the teacher taking me over the cobbled road to the church from the infants school. There we were met by Father McIntyre, the local parish priest at the time, and my mother. It took only about fifteen minutes, and I was then taken back to my class.

I also made my first Holy Communion in that church. I remember we had a trial run a while before, and were all lined up on the altar steps. As I walked back up the aisle to my seat, I was horrified to find I had bitten into the host and broken it. I dared not tell anyone, and I dared not tell Miss Ledwich that I had done so. She would have gone spare, throwing one of the usual, red-faced, spitting, fist-clenching, foot-stamping fits that she was so well known for. It was quite a while later that I realised we'd only been given a Trebor mint on that occasion. And woe betide any of us kids if we did not show for nine o'clock mass on Sundays. Miss Ledwich was always there at nine, and it caused quite a few arguments when my parents went to the school to tell her to mind her own business about whatever time they sent their kids to mass.

Father Murphy was one of the clergy at St Mary's. We'd always see him walking out from the vestry, the pulpit, or the old confessional box at the back of the church. There was a candle stand where we used to get half-burnt candles, but we used them to polish the slide on the Red Rec.

I can remember on Sundays the comforting sound of the church bell could be heard echoing all over Bridgefield. How I miss the sound of those church bells on a Sunday these days. St Mary's Church on Dodge Hill had a single note bell that I could hear from my house, and all over Bridgefield Street. The air stood silent, and all I could hear was that bell and the ones from the other churches around Stockport. I loved the sound as it signalled a day of rest, a day of peace, a day for sitting down with the family for Sunday dinner. Sunday was my favourite day. There were no shops open and even Prince's Street was silent. There was no sound of the mills working, or anything else for that matter. There was no school for us kids, so we all had a lie-in. It was a lazy day for all the family to be together. What a peaceful day it was.

One of my mother's saying that she used a lot was 'Kids should be seen and not heard'. One thing she didn't realise though, was that we kids heard and saw everything, and had many tales to tell.

WASH DAY

Bann Street public wash house.

As I walk round the streets of Stockport today, I look up Bridgefield Street and I can see my mam and me in the distance walking up the street with a pram laden with washing. I see myself holding on to the pram handle as Mother and I make our way towards Bann Street public wash house. The usual mode of transport then for many a housewife was the pram. Besides moving little toddlers around, they were used for taking the washing to the public wash house, or for getting the shopping home, even for picking up the odd bag of coal. Many a time I saw the odd stick of furniture, from a chest of drawers to a bed, being moved around the estate on prams. What a useful tool it was. My mother always took a pram in those days to get things home. Although I would have the pleasure of being pushed around part of the way, by the time the shopping was done there was no room left for me and I always finished up walking home.

Wash day in the 1950s was a chore not relished by most housewives, as it took up almost the whole day, and it was hard work. Monday always seemed to be designated as the day for it.

Mother would kick us out of bed at seven in the morning, then strip off the blankets and bundle them into the pram. There'd be a packet of Omo or Tide tucked in with the washing, a couple of blocks of green Fairy washing soap, a scrubbing brush and a bottle of Lanry or Melry bleach. We then made our way down Heaton Lane, onto King Street, then onto Bann Street.

The wash house fascinated me as a kid. It was full of wonderful, antiquated technology like hissing steam pipes, clanging metal doors and whirring motors. And the local women talking in loud voices. Although I was never allowed in the wash house part, I could sit on the bench inside and Mother bought me a penny hot Bovril or Oxo.

I remember the local women with their turbans on. Their sleeves would be rolled up to their armpits, and the front of their pinafores would be dripping wet. They constantly wiped their brows as they slaved away at the hot steaming boilers. The smell of soap, bleach and fresh clean washing wafted through the wash house air, and has stayed with me to this day.

Once Mother had finished at the boilers and spinner, she would take the washing to the drying room where it was put into long pull-out drying cabinets, or horses as they called them. After about an hour's drying time, we folded it up, placed it in the pram then made our way back home. By this time, it was mid-afternoon and we'd call at the UCP at the top of Prince's Street for a bag of chips for me. Fantastic chips, the best chips I can ever remember eating.

On arriving home, the washing was hung on the line in the courtyard to air a little before going back on the bed. Walk into any of those courtyards on a Monday and you would see lines full of washing blowing in the breeze. They were busy little areas as the housewife would be hanging out the washing, having a natter with the neighbour, or stoning the back step.

Sometimes my mother did every stage of the wash at home. Out came the dolly tub, and the posser for swirling the washing round with. Dolly Blue was put in for whitening all the white shirts. I used to love dissolving those Dolly Blue bags, swishing them around and squashing them in the tub until I was left with just the empty bag and peg, and of course the blue fingers.

Then it was off with the cover, over the mangle in the yard, and time for us to both get wet through this time. I was always nominated to crank the handle of the mangle while Mum fed the washing through the wooden rollers. Not everyone could afford a mangle, but those that could do usually kept it covered up outside the back door along with the tin bath. Anybody that wanted to use a mangle only had to ask the owner. I saw many a housewife toiling away, pushing the wet clothes though the wooden rollers, with a bored-looking kid who would rather be playing out with us, cranking away on the handle for their mother. The times poor Mum trapped her fingers in those rollers - ouch! wasn't the word she used.

Before the whites had time to dry on the line, it was out with the flat iron and onto the gas hob to heat up, no electric irons for us then. After the ironing was done, it was time to start the tea.

What a way to spend a day! Hoovers were around then, but the washers were nothing like they are today, and were unaffordable for many. So next time we switch on those labour-and-time-saving devices, give a thought to our parents, who had no such luxuries. Life is so simple now: just plug in, switch on and put your feet up.

The forties and fifties were lean times, but despite all the hard work, life was taken at a leisurely pace. There was no hustle and bustle like there is today. People had time for each other and would always find a moment to sit and have a chat. What a community we lived in! It had its ups and downs, but even days at the wash house are ones I shall always remember.

CHAOS THE WHOLE TIME

The Prince's Picture Palace on Prince's Street.

I have wonderful memories of the childhood that I spent in Old Stockport Town. They were hard times, but I loved every minute that I spent in the slums as a kid, and I wouldn't change it for the world. If I had my time again, I would take those very same steps as before.

In the 1950s we didn't have the entertainment that today's kids have. Going to the sixpenny Saturday matinee at the Plaza cinema was our favourite. All those wonderful films: *Roy Rogers, The Lone Ranger, Batman and Robin, Laurel and Hardy, The Three Stooges with Larry, Mo and Joe*, and all the Disney cartoons.

We used to get some live entertainment half-way through the show, when there was wrestling. I remember one of the wrestlers wore a red mask and his opponent was always trying to take his mask off. All the kids were cheering him on, thinking something sinister was about to be revealed, but it never was. Or there was some chap on stage with a yo-yo who kept the kids amused with the amazing tricks he used to do with it. Or there was a 'twister' - someone who made animals with long balloons.

It was chaos the whole time. When we were queuing outside, Peg Leg would try to keep hundreds of noisy and unruly kids in order, then he'd be shouting and prodding them with his walking cane until the show had finished. Then the great Wurlitzer organ would rise from the centre of the stage and we would sing along with the words scrolling up on the screen. When the show was over, all the kids stood for the national anthem, not in respect for queen or country, but to make a mad dash for the door. Then it was time for the stampede to the exit. Dozens of excited little hooligans were let loose into Mersey Square, jumping around on the Plaza steps, acting out Batman and Robin or playing at cowboys and injuns.

I am glad to have been born in the 1940s. I have watched the changing face of Stockport over the years and I have seen the advance of the technology we have today. There were no TVs back then, as you had to be rich to have one of those. The only piece of modern technology I owned then was a crystal radio set that did not need electricity or batteries to operate it; we didn't have leccy anyway and batteries were too expensive. We sat many a night listening to the radio in the bedroom. There were two earphones, one left, one right, that we would pass around between us. There wasn't much else to do on the dark nights of winter. Having no electric meant we had to read our books and comics, or play our indoor games, by gaslight. Mostly though, we used our imagination and flair and made our own entertainment.

During the day, we played out in all kinds of weather and always made the most of it, only coming home when hungry. We'd be out for hours on the Red Rec, making daisy chains, swinging on the trees, collecting caterpillars, playing on the football pitch. Despite all its rundown, ramshackle and crumbling houses, we kids just saw Stockport as a big adventure playground waiting to be explored. The railways, the River Mersey and the local tip on Lanky Hill were a treasure trove to us kids. We found many a useful thing to play with on the tip: wheels to make raggers out of, and toys that had been thrown away, we made good use of them all.

When not at school, we spent very little time indoors. Rain or shine, we always played out. On summer days, we would always be outside. If you were lucky enough to own a complete bike, we thought you were rich. A few of us had basic ones cannibalised from old bike bits. With a frame and two wheels, we were ready to go, and we didn't think lights, brakes and mudguards existed then.

If we weren't playing on the Red Rec, the red rocks or down by the Mersey River, we would be in the Great Egerton Street air raid shelters where we had our den. We'd spend many an hour in them. Most of the shelters have been replaced by the M60 motorway, but from what I remember, they used to run under Stewart Street and to the other side of the A6. But we were never brave enough to venture that far in the pitch black with just candles.

The entrance to the shelters that we used most often was between Brown Street and Robin Court where I lived. I remember it had a green wooden door built into the red rocks, and I was later told it was also a medical outpost during the war. Mum and Dad had used that entrance as it was literally two doors away. The entrance was right there when the air raid siren sounded.

We found many things in the tunnels that had been left by those sheltering from the air raids a few years before: old gas masks, bottles, clothes, bedding, shoes and rusty tins. Pennies, ha'pennies and thre'penny bits were a common find. There was also another entrance on Port Street, and one just below Stewart Street opposite the bookies in the rag merchants on Broady's yard.

I remember the siren on the school canteen roof on Great Egerton Street. Long after the war, these sirens were sounded periodically, to test them to make sure they were still working properly. It used to frighten the oldies som'at awful.

There was also a short tunnel that went from Brown Street under Harry Slacks and came out onto the East Cheshire railway line that ran from Tiviot Dale and through Stockport. I shudder now when I realise the danger we put ourselves in. We used to go on that railway to place washers and pennies on the line and watch the trains run over them.

We always found something to do. I remember standing at the slaughterhouse door of Harry Slacks on Stewart Street watching the slaughter man at work with some poor animal that had met its end there. A bit gruesome I know, but the men knew we were there, and they never closed the door. The smell was awful! We found the empty shells from the bolt gun to use as whistles, not realising then, as kids, what they were actually used for.

On nice days we would go fishing in the Lanky Cut on Wharf Street, Heaton Norris. Just behind Sheffield Street is where the canal came to an end and there was a sunken barge there that we climbed on to play. We would travel way beyond Nelstrops flour mill fishing for stickle backs and newts. Fishing nets were sixpence from Woollies, but we didn't have a tanner to spare. Instead, we improvised with one of Mother's old nylons, a piece of wire and a bamboo cane, with a jam jar to put our catch in. We'd also play down on the slippy, muddy banks of the River Mersey.

During the school holidays, Mother would send us off to the Red Rec with two brush stales (broom handles), an old woolly blanket and a ball of string, and that was our makeshift tent for the day. We'd go round collecting some twigs to make a campfire. Mother supplied us with two tins of beans to warm up on the fire. It was never successful, but it was fun trying. The empty tins were then washed out and string attached to make our 'phone' go from one tent to the other.

We'd sometimes take our homemade bows and arrows, made from privet hedge twigs, debarked. Or if it was conker time, we'd be at the top of the tree where the tantalising big ones hung leering at us as we threw sticks at them to bring them down to ground level. If someone took a ball, we were really made up for the day. Give the girls a stick of chalk and a tin of Mansion polish, a clean pavement, three balls and a skipping rope, and they were as happy as Larry too. It kept them away from us. We were men, not wishing to be seen as cissies playing with girls.

Of course, we'd take a picnic with us. That consisted of butties wrapped up in the greaseproof paper that the bread came in. A butty would be a slice of bread buttered on one side with marg, which we would dip butter-side down in the sugar basin so the sugar stuck to it. Other butties we could make were with condensed milk, or syrup, or dripping if there was any left in the cup, or jam. I always offered my mates one. I remember the bread was Mothers Pride, or Champion. We'd also take two Jusoda or Tizer bottles filled with water, which we could refill in the park's drinking fountain, and maybe a bottle of sterilized milk and a bottle opener.

We'd spend most of the day outside, just going home now and again for another butty. I remember the Ogdens that lived on Great Egerton Street. Raymond was one of my playmates and one sunny day he called at our house. He put his hand in his pocket and pulled out a wad of pound notes, around eight to ten of them. I asked him where he'd got them from as I'd never seen so much money before. He said it was his birthday and he'd got it from relatives. I didn't ask any more questions and when Raymond asked me to go and spend it with him, I did. Our first call was the sweet shops, then on to Woolworths.

In Woollies we bought a teepee. We then spent an hour or two on the Red Rec erecting this teepee and playing in it till we got bored. As we were about to leave, a couple of kids came up to us. They were quite intrigued with the teepee, so we told them they could have it, and then we left.

We walked down the Rec Brow and along Stewart Street stuffing our faces with the sweets and grub we'd bought. We'd just got to the bottom of the steps on Brown Street when Raymond's grandad grabbed him, threw him over his shoulder and carted him off home. When I went home, I got a right rollicking too. My mother tipped out my pockets to see if Raymond had given me any of this money, but thankfully he hadn't. Mother then told me where he had got it from. Naughty Raymond had stolen it off his grandma.

More often than not, we'd go home as black as the ace of spades. Many of the kids walked around with holes in their shoes, just as I did. On many occasions I remember cutting out pieces of Lino to fit in the bottom of my shoe. It lasted longer. We kids were angels with dirty faces and grubby little mitts. We wore hand-me-down clothing that was always a size too big. We had scuffed up shoes, scraped and bloodied knees, and socks around our ankles. But our cheeky little grins won the hearts of many as we played on the dusty streets in this grimy cotton mill town.

I DIDN'T KNOW WHO THE QUEEN WAS

The Goodwill Christmas tree at the Bear Pit on Mersey Square, with the old fire station in the background.

The Coronation was over six decades ago now, but it doesn't seem that long. I remember it well. I was only a nipper then and I didn't know who the Queen was or what she did. But it became a talking point with many of the residents at the time.

The day of 2 June 1953 was warm but overcast in Stockport. I remember the coloured bunting stretched across Prince's Street and other surrounding streets. I watched the residents zigzag the bunting along Great Egerton Street from their bedroom windows. They didn't need ladders, they just passed it up to the windows with a clothes prop. On the day, residents brought out their tables and chairs. The tables were placed down the middle of the cobbled streets and loaded with goodies. There was no need to worry about traffic then, as there was hardly any.

I remember my mam making platefuls of potted beef butties for the kids, and it was tongue and brawn for the grownups. I also remember her spending most of the night before baking jam tarts in the living room on the dinner table, as we didn't have a kitchen.

Everyone would chip in with whatever they could afford to give, to make it a memorable day for us kids. Pop flowed like the River Mersey. Butter and sugar and a lot of other things were still on ration and were hard to get hold of, so you were very careful with what little you did have. Sugar was a commodity that was particularly difficult to get hold of. But just before the Coronation, the government released many thousands of tons into the confectionery trade. Well, I was happy with that, because it meant that now sweets and chocolate became abundant in the shops.

Joe Broad, the rag merchant on Great Egerton Street, was a good kind-hearted man who did a lot for the community around there at the time. I remember Mother saying to me that he had the job of handing out 'coronation glasses' to all the Bridgefield residents. "Go across to the stables and see if you can get one," said Mum. So I did. I remember Joe was stood there handing out bags of sweets to the kids. Well, I was more interested in the sweets than the fancy glasses.

There was an old woman sat on a chair beside Joe, in front of a wall of musty-smelling rags piled up behind her. I took this to be his mother, and the old dear gave me a glass and told me not to drop it on my way home. Joe gave me the biggest bag of sweets I'd ever seen, Liquorish Allsorts they were.

I ran home clutching this glass because I couldn't hold the glass and eat my sweets at the same time. I remember Mother saying, "It's really beautiful. Go and see if you can get another." I hid my bag of sweets in the drawer as I didn't want anyone getting their mitts on my rare treasures.

Back up Egerton Street and into the stables where Joe kept the horse and carts, I stood at the back of the queue until I came to the front again. Needless to say, I got another glass and another bag of sweets off Joe. I had never seen so many sweets in my life, and now I had two bags to share with my sibs.

There were also treats for us every Christmas although in the fifties it didn't start anywhere near as early as it does today. We would get really excited about putting the decorations up but our mum would only give us the go-ahead about a week before the big day. We, as kids, were always actively involved in decorating the Christmas tree and the room to our liking. Despite the prevailing arguments, we would make our own decorations to hang around the ceiling from flat sheets of coloured crepe paper cut into two- to three-inch strips. We twisted them as we unwound them and draped tinsel over them. I loved the way the tinsel used to sparkle in the dim glow of the gaslight in the room at night. I remember just how magical Christmas was as a kid.

Although money was always tight and we never got exactly what we wanted, our parents always did their best. My parents always had a much needed helping hand at Christmas from charities like the Good Will Christmas Tree which used to stand in the Bear Pit on Mersey Square. This was a charitable organisation run by Stockport Round Table. It was our parents' saviour at Christmas with four kids to look after at such an expensive time. Once the tree had been put up, just before Christmas, we'd go to Mersey Square, climb onto the balustrade around the Bear Pit and sit listening to the Christmas carols echoing around the square from the loudspeakers. We'd watch people throw money into the large conical-shaped containers down below. The good people of Stockport also brought in their unwanted presents, ready-wrapped or just in bags, to give to the waiting organisers. The toys were distributed among the poor families around the town. Our family was one of those that benefited from the generosity of the people of Stockport. Those people made a considerable difference and brought a smile to many a child's face on Christmas Day. Without their generosity, Christmas Days for some of those kids would have been a lot more sombre and cold than they were.

Christmastime on the market was always magical, especially for us kids. Christmas trees were decked out with tinsel, and stalls were piled high with apples and oranges. These were a rare sight in those days, as most fruit was still on ration from the war years. It was better than any Santa's grotto.

We could hardly get near the toy stalls for the crowds and as I waited there with Mother, my fingers and toes turned blue on those cold December days. The toys Mother bought on the market for Christmas were never for me, or so she said, they were always for my brother or sisters. I was sworn to secrecy not to tell, but I wondered on Christmas Day why I ended up with some of those secrets I was meant to keep.

Birthdays and Christmases were always difficult times for our parents, but they did their best every time. Mother would rob Peter to pay Paul to get those little bits of presents and extra food for us. The tallyman on a Friday night would be the first casualty and would get the silent treatment when knocking on the door.

Christmas Eve was one of the rare occasions Dad would put a fire in the upstairs fire grate. Mum and Dad always stayed up on this night getting things ready to make the next day special. Dad got the meat ready to cook while Mum did her baking on the dining table. All night long we could smell the roast, and Mum baking her mince pies and apple pies. What wonderful aromas I remember.

We could hear Mum clattering her pots and pans about. The heat from the downstairs open fire and gas cooker would rise up the staircase and into the bedroom, making the bedroom even warmer. We lay in bed watching the shadows from the flickering fire dancing on the ceiling, far too excited to go to sleep. But as the night grew on into the early hours of the morning, we could no longer stay awake, and would fall asleep.

The first one awake next morning would tell everyone the toys were there. On Christmas Day, we always woke up to a pile of second-hand toys. One year, I got the cowboy suit I so badly wanted from my parents, and I was made up just like my hero Roy Rogers. I donned the suit, and as I stepped outside on that cold December morning in 1954, the snow was ankle deep and not a footprint was to be seen anywhere. I made my way up the ginnel onto Brown Street and not a living soul could be seen or heard. There was also not even a bird in the sky that I could shoot with my new hundred-shot repeater rifle.

Among the presents I often got from the tree were annuals, jigsaws, a compendium of games, a box of magic tricks and a few obviously used cars. All of them were used, but they were normally complete and in good condition. It didn't matter that they weren't new, and we were really grateful for what we received. I never did get the chance to thank the good people of Stockport for their generosity. I may be sixty years late to thank them but without those kind people, Christmas Days would have been a lot bleaker than they were. Things like oranges and nuts were considered a luxury in those days, due to the cost and to not being readily available, and they were also a major part of the Christmas presents in my stocking.

Mum shouted us down for breakfast and one by one we'd stroll downstairs. This was the one morning we never saw porridge. Bacon, egg, fried bread, grilled sausage and tomatoes were on the table that day. Mum pulled the plates out of the side oven of the open fireplace where they were keeping warm, and placed them on the table. A mound of toast sat on a plate in the middle under the gaslight. As Mum was getting out the hot plates, we all sat in awe and looked at the glittering Christmas tree stood in the corner of the room. The glass ornaments glittered as they caught the light of the gas lamp. The lametta and the decorations hanging around the ceiling swayed gently in the warm air.

Straight after breakfast, we would wrap up well then head outside to go to the church on the hill. Mother was a staunch Catholic but all we wanted to do was stay in and play. After church, we ran down the Rec Brow, so we could get back to the lovely warm house and carry on playing with our toys for the day. That day was for the family, and I remember it well.

The atmosphere in our old house on Christmas Day was amazing: the heat, the warmth, the table laid for a special dinner. Dinner was the traditional roast and vegetables. Christmas pudding with white sauce came after.

Tea was cold meat on a plate that you could make into sandwiches yourself if you wanted to, with the usual jelly and tinned fruit with Carnation milk for afters. Boxes of dates, bowls of fresh fruit and baskets of mixed nuts lay on the table where the Christmas tree stood. We'd spend many an hour cracking open the nuts.

With each and every year that passes, my family grows bigger and my pockets grow smaller. But I love Christmastime as it is the only time the whole family comes together in the same place at the same time. However, as the years pass, I now feel sad that the younger generation of today seems to be losing the true meaning of Christmas. The kids know it has something to do with Jesus Christ, but not many could tell you what. We have allowed it to become far too commercialised. I seem to remember that Christmas was to celebrate the birth of Christ, not the birth of internet shopping. It's not to honour who can spend the most, or who gets the most expensive gadgets. I remember how magical Christmas was as a kid. Although life was hard, and money was always tight with everyone, and we didn't always get what we wanted, we were always happy with what we were given. It was all so much better than the consumerism we have created today. What a life it was. One I loved so much. Sometimes I still wish it was like that, because I would still be there.

TRAGIC CIRCUMSTANCES

A tram on Mersey Square, 1940s.

It makes me wonder sometimes just how we managed to get by in the slums of 1950s Stockport. Life was not as easy as it is now. Some times were good but there were bad times as well. Some of the times I remember would give a kid nightmares for years to come.

One very sad day indeed was in the summer of 1954 when one of my little playmates went under the wheels of the Number 30 bus. This was on the zebra crossing on Merseyway, just outside Woolworths, where Union Bridge joined Union Road. The traffic was light in those days and there was not much of it around. However, on this particular day little Johnny was left on the Union Bridge side of Merseyway as the others dashed across. Little Johnny dithered for a moment and was left alone stood on the kerb. He then made a sudden dash across, only to be hit by a bus. Killed outright.

I remember the day of the funeral. It was a very sad, solemn occasion, and most of the residents of the Bridgefield estate turned out as a mark of respect for him and his mother. I stood in silence with my mother, as did everyone else. Little Johnny lived in Green's Place and, with tears in our eyes, we stood opposite there as the cars arrived. His tiny white coffin was placed on the back parcel shelf of the undertaker's car. I watched as his mother, dressed in black, walked up Green's Place, flanked by two of the undertakers, towards the cars parked on Woodman Street.

Everybody stood in complete silence. The street was lined with residents who had turned out to pay their last respects to a little boy who had lost his life in such tragic circumstances. The cars made their way slowly along Great Egerton Street towards the A6, then turned left and were out of sight. This is something that has haunted me for many years, and my eyes still well up even now when I think about my little playmate Johnny, who was only three years old.

Another incident I recall around the summer of 1955 was when the 'New Mills Murderess' came into our house. I was sat at the dining table eating some biscuits in our one-up one-down house in Robin Court. The front door was open, as it was a warm sunny day. I sat facing the door and could see out over the courtyard. I looked up as I heard the footsteps and the sobbing and wailing of a woman in distress. She was being led by the arm across the yard by my aunt, Anne Wood, a relative of ours who lived in the same courtyard as we did.

Anne had been to the shops near Mersey Square and had come across this woman in a distressed and confused state as she wandered down Prince's Street. Not realising why, or what the woman had done that very morning, Anne brought her home to our house for a cup of tea, and to try and calm her down a little.

Aunty Anne helped the woman up the doorstep into the house and sat her down in the only armchair we had. The woman sat in the chair rocking back and forth with her head in hands.

"Oh, my Michael, my Michael, what have I done?" she cried. I saw Mother mouth to Aunty Anne, "What's up with her?" Anne shrugged her shoulders and spread her hands as if to gesture, 'I've no idea'.

Mother then poured the woman a cup of tea and took it over to her. She was still rocking back and forth, so Mother gently asked what the matter was. The woman looked up at Mother and screamed so loud it feared me to death! I leaped off my chair and ran to hide in the coal hole under the stairs. Mother and Anne were taken aback and tried to console her.

"What's wrong with Michael?" Mother asked. The woman stopped rocking and looked very steely eyed at Mother.

"He's dead. I've just murdered him." I will spare you the gory details of what she said after that, but the words she uttered shocked me as a kid. I have never forgotten them to this day.

"Where is Michael now?" Mother asked.

"He's at home, on the table."

Apparently, she had killed her son and laid him out on the table, and surrounded his body by lit candles, before boarding a bus from New Mills to Mersey Square. Michael was just fourteen years old at the time.

Then the woman suddenly grabbed my sister Katherine by the arm and pulled her over to her.

"What is your name?" she asked.

"Kathy," was the reply.

"I have a little girl called Kathy," she said. Mother, realising this was not a good situation to be in, grabbed Kathy by the collar and pulled her away. She then pushed her behind her well out of the woman's reach.

Mother finally recovered from the shock of what she had just been told. "For crying out loud, Anne, take her out and give her to the first policeman you see!" Anne walked the woman along Brown Street to Prince's Street, and duly handed her over to a policeman on the beat.

I remember the following day. Dad sent me for a newspaper to the vendor who used to walk along Prince's Street selling them. I remember looking at the headlines and pictures in *The Evening Chronicle* and seeing that the story had made front page news. The outcome of the case was that the woman was eventually declared insane and was 'detained at Her Majesty's pleasure'.

I loved every minute of the time I spent in the slums as a kid, and I wouldn't change it for the world. If I had my time again, I would take those very same steps again, only this time I'd tread more carefully.

COMPULSORY PURCHASE ORDER

Slum clearance of Great Egerton Street.

Although Bridgefield was a slum area, and it was declared unfit for human habitation in the 1940s, Compulsory Purchase Orders were only issued in the early fifties. Many of the houses were falling down and in great need of replacing. None had bathrooms, inside toilets, running hot water or, in many cases, even electricity. I remember my parents talking about the compulsory purchase around 1955. My Mum was standing by the open fire with her glasses raised, and the letter turned towards the brighter light of the flames, reading to Dad the compulsory purchase order letter we'd received. We were one of the first to receive the letter confirming our house was to come under that order.

The CPO order was enforced in 1956 and that was when the slum clearance got underway. It was a very sad time indeed, as I stood with a heavy heart and a tear in my eye watching the streets and courtyards of my youth disappear under the enormous strength of the bulldozers. I watched as the demolition men put chains around the old houses. I watched the houses fall into piles of brick and dust. I saw them pulling the heart out of Stockport.

Many of the residents were put into new high-rise flats, some on the Red Rec up at Lancashire Hill. I remember the building of those flats, as they took away the playground that I had spent so many hours on. And that pile-driving drove us all daft for months. However, the flats eventually proved to be very unpopular with many people, particularly the older generation of the time. The old, terraced houses may have been grim, but at least they had a strong sense of community.

Many of the residents of Bridgefield were moving from a place they'd spent their whole lives in, and were probably born in, like myself. We were moving to places where nobody knew anyone: we didn't know them, and they didn't know us. But times change, and we have to move with those times whether we like it or not.

Three years later in 1959, we were one of the first residents to move to Heaton Norris. On the day of the 'flit' (flitting was the common word used then for someone moving house) there was not a lot to go from the old house to the new one. We had very few possessions then, as the old house was only a one-up and one-down. Mainly there were just the beds, and what little furniture there was in the downstairs room. The council moved us, and the larger items were first taken somewhere to be fumigated. As they were coming from the slums, the council didn't want us taking any uninvited guests along with us to the new property.

With the smaller items, like pots and pans, I remember my brother and me walking up Wellington Road passing Christ Church and going over Belmont Bridge with a pram full of bits and pieces, and then going back for more knick-knacks till the old house was empty. I took one last look around and said goodbye to the place that held so many childhood memories.

We waited at the new house nearly all day for the furniture to arrive back from fumigation. While we waited, we explored our new surroundings. We ran round and round in the immense space we now had at our disposal, deciding who was having which bedroom. We had been used to living in a very confined space, but this house was much bigger than the one we were used to in the slums. It had three rooms downstairs, three rooms upstairs and two hallways - a grand palace compared to the cramped conditions we had been so used to for all those years.

We also now had a house with electricity, and I thought this new-fangled electricity thing was a wonderful invention. We could light a room up, or darken it instantly, with the flick of a switch, no matches or candles required. It was a novelty, and we went from room to room, flicking switches on and off. We had sockets as well, but nothing to plug into them just yet. How I wanted to see how these things worked.

However, we'd basically just moved from one slum to another. The new house didn't have an inside toilet or bathroom, it had no running hot water and there was no heating other than a large open cast-iron grate, just like the one in the old house. But at least the outside toilet was in our own little back yard and wasn't shared.

Although I thought it was a long way from Heaton Norris to Bridgefield, I'd still go back after school and at weekends to hang around with a few of my old playmates that still lived on Bridgefield but were just waiting to be moved. Only this time it was a much longer walk back home than when I lived there too. If I had a penny, I could catch a number 92 or 89 bus to Belmont Bridge from Mersey Square.

I remember going back and walking around the old streets where I was born. What a harrowing experience that was! I gingerly ventured down the ginnel into the courtyard I knew so well. Robin Court, where I was born and had lived for ten years of my life, was empty and derelict. What a sad sight. That courtyard used to be so full of life. The little hive of community that I'd known so well, which had been full of pride and warmth, was now cold, empty and uninviting.

I heard voices as I walked slowly past the yellow front door of the old house, which had been painted by my Dad, and tried to gaze in. It seemed as if someone was actually living in our house, strange as it seemed, but maybe they were squatters, I never knew. Maybe if I'd had a glass like Mother used, I would have heard a little more. When Mother noticed a row starting next door, she would get out a glass and put it against the wall to magnify the sound. At the same time, she would give Dad a running commentary on what was being said, a bit more gossip for the neighbours to spread around tomorrow.

The streets I had played on, the house I had started life in, those quaint little corner shops where I would spend my pennies, the houses of my friends and playmates, now stood like empty shells, devoid of all human life. Houses were empty, with no rooves, windows or doors. An eerie silence fell over the scene of devastation.

They were slums, but I didn't know that then. All I knew then was that it was my home, my town. It wasn't a sight for the faint-hearted as my hometown was bulldozed into something that resembled a war zone. I watched the houses fall into piles of bricks and dust. Those communities had been the lifeblood of Stockport town centre, and had kept its heart beating until the early 1960s. When the Council moved the residents out, that heart was slowly bled dry.

It had been a dark, damp, dismal house. But I loved it, and it was a family home. All the friends and the neighbours I knew were now dispersed far afield across Stockport. We had lived our lives together, played together, worked together. Everyone knew everyone and their business, and they knew us. We knew every nook and cranny around the Bridgefield estate. Times were lean, and very hard. Many a time I saw Mother with her head in her hands crying about how she was going to put food on the table for us kids. Many a time my parents found it hard to manage, but we got by. People all mucked in with one another and helped out. It had that wartime feeling of where everyone rallied together, and there was a great feeling of social cohesion in the community.

The Bridgefield estate was finally confined to the realms of the history books and the memories of oldies like myself who remember and lived there. But my past lives on in this book.

THINGS WE CAN NOT EXPLAIN

St Mary's on Dodge Hill.

We grew up in a much safer environment than we can ever imagine these days. Children were allowed to be children, and were able to enjoy the freedom of the outdoor life in complete safety. There was no such thing as health and safety in those days. And yet, there were sometimes things that made our mothers really worry.

From being a kid, I have never really believed in ghosts, ghouls or that awful bogey man Mother tried to frighten us with. Many of us have had many unexplained things happen to us in the past, but we just shrug our shoulders as we have no explanation for them. But one incident that I remember, many years ago, left me in no doubt that some things beyond our understanding do happen. There are things that we cannot account for, and we cannot explain.

This story culminated when I was well into my teens, around 1965. But the beginning of the story takes me back to 1955. There wasn't a great deal of entertainment in those days for the grownups, no TVs or anything like that other than the picture houses, or the local pubs. My dad liked his drink, but Mother never bothered that much and went out only occasionally with Dad to one of the local pubs on Great Egerton Street.

This particular Saturday night in 1955, both parents had gone out and my Aunt Francis was babysitting for us. As the night was coming to an end, the landlord called time, as was the rule in those days when pubs closed at 10.30 to 11.00 pm. Mum and Dad were the last two people to leave. The landlord (we'll call him Harry) waited for them to drink up before letting them out onto Great Egerton Street.

As my parents walked down the corridor from the bar, Harry followed them. They stepped out onto Great Egerton Street and said good night, then Harry closed the door behind them. They heard the bolts slide on, and as they started to walk away heard a muffled thump behind the door. Thinking nothing of it they started for home, a two-minute walk over the road to the gas-lit side street and into the courtyard where we lived.

The following morning, word got about that Harry had died the night before. Mum and Dad were shocked and could not believe it, as they had only said good night to him a few hours earlier. He had seemed fine then. But it later transpired that

Harry's wife Nelly had found him slumped behind the front door. She'd heard him bolt the door, and waited for him to come upstairs. After a while there was still no sign of him. Nelly thought he was finishing off in the bar and shouted down for him to leave it till the morning. There was no response, so she went down to see what Harry was doing, and found him dead behind the front door. That may have been the strange sound Mum and Dad had heard.

Nothing more was thought about it, and the funeral went as planned. Harry was laid to rest, or so we thought until ten years later when he paid us a visit at the new house we had moved to!

Nelly moved away shortly after Harry died, but we never knew where she had moved to. And we moved in 1959 from the slums of Bridgefield to a house in Heaton Norris.

Life went on as usual until one day around 1965, Mother was walking back from the post office when she heard a woman on the other side on the road calling, "Mary! Mary!" It took a moment for Mother to realise it was Nelly, whom she hadn't seen for almost ten years. Strangely, Nelly lived only four to five hundred yards away from us, and in all those years neither of them knew it until now.

The conversation went on for quite some time as they caught up on the gossip they'd missed out on for all those years. I sat on someone's garden wall kicking my heels waiting for Mother. I always remember as a kid one of Mother's sayings was 'Kids should be seen and not heard', but I don't think it ever meant we couldn't listen to what was being said.

Physically, Mam and Nelly were both about the same height and a little on the plump side. I remember hearing Nelly say she had quite a few dresses she was getting rid of, and asked

Mum if she wanted them. Mother immediately said yes. Nelly said some were what Harry had bought for her many years before, but after all this time she still couldn't bear to throw them out, and would rather see someone put them to good use. Nelly dropped them off at our house a few days later.

They had also arranged for a double bed to be delivered as well, one of Nelly's old ones. The girls needed a new bed, so it was gratefully accepted by Mother. Out went the old bed, and up went the new.

Towards the weekend, Mother had an appointment somewhere so she pulled out one of the dresses Nelly had given her. At bedtime, Mother laid the dress neatly over the back of an armchair in her bedroom. Mum and Dad had the back bedroom, although it was more of a box room as only one double bed and an armchair would fit in there.

In the morning, Mother got up to find the dress wasn't where she'd left it. Thinking nothing of it, she went down to make a brew. She waited till Dad got up before asking him if he had moved it.

"I've not seen any dress," he said. So after everyone had got up and sorted themselves out for work and school, Mother went upstairs looking for the dress she had neatly put out the night before. There was still no sign of it.

Later that morning, Mother's friend Betty called round. Mother told Betty about the strange experience of the missing dress.

"You're losing your marbles, Mary," she said. "Let's go and have a look." They both went upstairs and stripped the sheets off the bed and the cushions off the chair. No dress was found, so Mother got another one out.

"You must have been dreaming, Mary. Are you sure you did?" Mother then racked her brains all day. She knew where she had put it, but where had it gone?

Dad was a driver for a local firm now and on odd occasions would call home at dinner time and make a brew of tea to have with his sandwiches. This one particular day when he came back, no one was at home as everyone was out going about their business.

As Dad opened the front door, "I thought the banshees of hell had been let loose in the house," he said later. But nothing could be heard outside. He described the noise as being horrendous and thought the whole neighbourhood's kids were screaming and playing and jumping around upstairs.

He hurried down the lobby to the foot of the stairs, and shouted up, not mincing his words, "What the bloody hell is going on up there?" A deathly silence fell in the house, not a sound to be heard. He stormed upstairs expecting to find loads of kids misbehaving. The three bedrooms at the top of the stairs were serviced by a landing, and as Dad walked from one room to the other, there was no sign of anyone. After quickly peering under the beds and into the wardrobes thinking these kids must be hiding, Dad quickly turned on his heels, went downstairs and left the house. He never bothered going into the kitchen to make a brew.

On his way out, Dad met Mrs May from next door. He asked her if she had heard any noise or commotion coming from our house. "Not a sound," she said. So off he went back to work.

In the evening, as they were sat watching telly, Dad told Mother about the incident in the afternoon. Both then ended up telling each other about the strange things that they had kept experiencing around the house, like strange noises, things going missing and footsteps.

"I heard footsteps walking down the stairs the other night," said Mum.

"It was probably the old staircase creaking," replied Dad.

"I can tell the difference between a creak and continuous footsteps," she said. "I got out of bed and when I looked over the banister rail it stopped, but as I went back into the bedroom it carried on again. I thought it might have been one of the kids going down, but it was too heavy for a child. I checked all the beds, and the kids were asleep."

This went on for a few weeks. One day in the afternoon, Mother, Betty and I were sat in the living room. Mother and Betty were having a fag, a chinwag and a cup of tea. We all looked at each other in silence as we distinctly heard heavy footsteps walk across the lino-covered landing. "Who's upstairs?" Betty said in a quiet voice. "No one should be," was Mother's reply. This was the first time Betty had experienced the strange activity that had been going on in the house.

Betty grabbed the heavy poker from the fireplace, and we all rushed to the foot of the stairs. Betty called up, "Who's there?" but there was no reply. The footsteps carried on till they reached the end of the landing, then stopped. "Who is it? I'm coming up," she said.

Betty went up first, as she had the weapon, then Mother followed, and me being the gentleman I wasn't far behind. We searched all three bedrooms together, but we saw nothing. We had no idea what could have made those noisy footsteps. As we were walking back across the landing to go down, we almost jumped out of our skins!

"Oooooh, that feared me to bloody death!" Betty screamed.

"What did?" said Mother.

"It was your cat."

"Betty, we haven't got a cat," Mother declared. Neither Mother nor I had seen any cat, but Betty said it had run downstairs and along the lobby to the front door. We looked, but the door was shut. Nothing would have got through, and there was no cat in the lobby.

We came down again and sat in the living room. Betty said, "I think you need to move, Mary. It scares me, and I don't think I could live here." The following day, Mother walked over to St Mary's Church on Dodge Hill and spoke to one of the priests, Father McIntyre or Father Murphy.

He called round to the house the next day and as soon as he walked in, he sensed there was something not quite right, and he told Mother so. He didn't spell it out in so many words, but his eyes were all over, and we knew what he meant. Mother had asked him the day before if he could perform an exorcism as we had an unsettled soul wandering around the house.

"I cannot perform an exorcism in the house," he said, "as I am not qualified to undertake such a task. All I can do for the moment is bless this house, and I will make enquiries as to what the next move should be."

He proceeded to walk from room to room, blessing each in turn as he entered it. As he was about to leave, he stood talking a while to Mother at the front door. Mother told him what had been going on for the past few months and when it had all started happening.

"My advice to you," he said, "first of all, is to get rid of whatever this man's wife gave you. He is not happy about it."

The day after, Mother duly cleared everything out, the dresses and the bed. Nothing was ever heard again, and the house returned to normal.

Believe it or not, but it's a true story.

AFTERWORD by Christine Emmons, Harry's daughter

After the slum clearance, Dad and his family moved to Heaton Norris and resided at Heaton Road, where I believe they stayed until around 1968. He, along with his parents and siblings, shared a three-bedroomed house, each set of boys and girls having their own room and my gran and grandad having the other. There was no inside bathroom/toilet, but I can only imagine it was far different to what they had been used to prior to this.

My grandma now worked at Longfield Open Air School, cleaning and helping with school meals, where she remained until the school closed in 1968. The school had been obtained by Stockport Education Committee in 1929, and was used as an open air school for children in town who suffered ill health, mainly through smoke pollution. My aunty attended that school due to a cleft palate, and it's now known as Tithe Barn Primary school.

I don't really know much about my grandad, and I've probably learned more about him from reading this book than I ever knew before. He was always a quiet, reserved chap who didn't hold much of a conversation. I do remember that when I was eight years old, I was in quite a bad car crash which left a permanent scar on my left cheek. Grandad gave me a doll to cheer me up, which I later left at Dad's house when I moved out. I remember it being a porcelain doll wearing a green dress, quite an ugly scraggy-looking thing, but nevertheless it was a present that was given to me. Dad always assured me he still had it, but I'm yet to discover where he may have put it. He had a habit of keeping things 'safe', did Dad. I had a three-wheeled tricycle when I was younger, which I kept riding in the road, that was until Dad took the front wheel off and said it had been pinched. We found that wheel in his shed a few years ago! It was never pinched and he'd just taken it off to keep me safe.

One of Dad's first jobs was working in the UCP café on Princess Street. He took those skills in later years to the Alma Lodge on Wellington Road where he worked as a breakfast chef. After the UCP café he worked at the hat works on Wellington Road as a maintenance man. He used to tell us how he would take his sandwiches and sit on top of the building looking across Stockport whilst he ate his lunch. He couldn't have stomached that in later life as he became quite scared of heights!

In 1968, Dad and his family moved to Reddish where he remained for the rest of his life. In 1971, he met my mum through a mutual acquaintance, and they married in on 4th May 1974 (World Cup day). In 1975, my sister Julie arrived, followed shortly after by me in 1977.

Dad had many jobs over the years and could put his hand to anything. He started the journey of becoming his own boss in 1987, opening a domestic appliance shop on Hyde Road, Gorton. The shop is no longer there, but the café next door still stands. He took us there one evening, my mum, my sister and me, and as we stood outside the door of the shop, he gave us each a shovel. 'When I open the door,' he said, 'if it moves, hit it! But don't hit your sister or your mother.' The shop was infested with rats, thousands of them. He eventually stood defeated and called in the pest control as there were just too many rats to get rid of by ourselves. It was very expensive for the pest control people to dispose of the bodies back then, so Dad took them home and buried them in his back garden…as you do!

Dad then moved his business to Fairfield Road in Openshaw, which is where he really made things work. He would leave the house before 6 am, then Mum would get us ready for school. However, Dad would always get me up around 5:30 am to make sure I watched *The Flintstones* with him before we started the day. Mum would then join him at the shop a little later. We never wanted for anything as kids, but we were never spoilt, far from it. If we asked for something, we did get it, but not without earning it first. My first experience of work was when I was ten years old on a Saturday cleaning the appliances ready to be sold in his shop. I stayed working for Dad at whatever point I could until 1992, when I had my first child. Since then I've always worked, managing to juggle ill health, three children and, in later years, looking after Dad. I owe my morals and way of life to him and what he taught us as kids: right from wrong, good from bad, and respect.

If my memory serves me correctly, Dad closed the shop around 1994. The main reason was the fact that people no longer required second-hand appliances due to the ability to order via a catalogue, or pay on the 'never never', as he called it.

After closing the shop, Dad briefly worked delivering fireplace mantels for a chap who lived at the bottom of his street. He finally retired in around 2006 at the age of about fifty-eight. Well, I say retired…in 2002 I met my husband who, at the time, was a hamster breeder. A few years after we met, I started working for Monarch Airlines, which opened up the world of travel for us. When we took our first holiday, we asked Dad to look after the hamsters whilst we were away, and he loved it. He looked after those animals with such love and care that my husband handed the business over to him. Dad sold the hamsters all over the country to various pet shops and people, building a website along the way which is still active today www.hammysworld.com. He moved the hamsters from the unit which housed them to a huge shed in his back garden, making it easier for him as he became poorly in later life.

My working for Monarch Airlines enabled us to travel all over the world for very little. We would travel standby almost every month to Lanzarote, which became Dad's favourite place. He always boasted to people how we'd managed to fly over there for less than what you'd pay for a meal out with the family.

Dad was the third of six siblings, but most passed away many years ago. His father, Alf, passed in 1990 at the age of sixty-seven. Mary, his mother, passed in 2002 at the age of seventy-six. His youngest brother Sean died in 1996, his sister Evelyn in 2001, his other sister Corrine, I'm not sure of, and his eldest brother Dereck in 2012. Dad and Cathy were the only two remaining for a number of years, that is until Dad's death in 2019.

Dad wanted to keep the memories of his childhood alive, not because he wanted sympathy for anything, as there would've been hundreds of families just like his, but because he didn't want people to forget the past and just how hard it was in those days. We, along with the people who started to read his stories, encouraged him to write everything down so people in years to come could read about how things were.

In 2014, Dad fell from a ladder whilst fixing a security light in his back garden and broke his hip. Whilst in hospital, they discovered that he had COPD and ischemic heart disease, and they told him his life would be limited. In 2015, he underwent a quintuple heart bypass at Manchester Royal Infirmary, which didn't cure his problems, but it helped for a while. In 2018, he became reliant on oxygen, and more dependent on myself and my sister to assist him in certain things. He never lost his independence, but he spent more and more time in hospital with various infections and problems. On the 23rd November 2019, Dad passed away peacefully in Stepping Hill Hospital with me, my sister and my daughter at his bedside. He was seventy-one years old.

145